THE BUSINESS PLAN COACH

Lindsey Byrne

The Teach Yourself series has been trusted around the world for over 60 years. It has helped millions of people to improve their skills and achieve their goals. This new 'Coach' series of business books is created especially for people who want to focus proactively on a specific workplace skill and to get a clear result at the end of it. Whereas many business books help you talk the talk, the Coach will help you walk the walk.

THE BUSINESS PLAN COACH

Lindsey Byrne

First published in Great Britain in 2014 by Hodder & Stoughton. An Hachette UK company.

First published in US in 2014 by The McGraw-Hill Companies, Inc.

This edition published 2014

Copyright © Lindsey Byrne 2014

The right of Lindsey Byrne to be identified as the Author of the Work has been asserted by her in accordance with the Copyright, Designs and Patents Act 1988.

Database right Hodder & Stoughton (makers)

The *Teach Yourself* name is a registered trademark of Hachette UK.

British Library Cataloguing in Publication Data: a catalogue record for this title is available from the British Library.

Library of Congress Catalog Card Number: on file.

10 9 8 7 6 5 4 3 2 1

The publisher has used its best endeavours to ensure that any website addresses referred to in this book are correct and active at the time of going to press. However, the publisher and the author have no responsibility for the websites and can make no guarantee that a site will remain live or that the content will remain relevant, decent or appropriate.

The publisher has made every effort to mark as such all words which it believes to be trademarks. The publisher should also like to make it clear that the presence of a word in the book, whether marked or unmarked, in no way affects its legal status as a trademark.

Every reasonable effort has been made by the publisher to trace the copyright holders of material in this book. Any errors or omissions should be notified in writing to the publisher, who will endeavour to rectify the situation for any reprints and future editions.

Cover image

Typeset by Cenveo® Publisher Services.

Printed and bound in Great Britain by CPI Group (UK) Ltd., Croydon, CRO 4YY.

Hodder & Stoughton policy is to use papers that are natural, renewable and recyclable products and made from wood grown in sustainable forests. The logging and manufacturing processes are expected to conform to the environmental regulations of the country of origin.

Hodder & Stoughton Ltd

338 Euston Road

London NW1 3BH

www.hodder.co.uk

Also available in ebook

DISCLAIMER

This book should not be used as a substitute for obtaining professional advice and input when planning a business venture. The content of this book is generic and, while suggestions are made on planning matters, readers are encouraged to contact professionally qualified tax accounting specialists and legal specialists to obtain advice specific to their circumstances.

This book also should be treated as an outline for information only in relation to the accounting chapters. For detailed information readers should refer to the relevant accounting standards published by the UK FRC, the IASB or the US FASB. This book does not contain advice on accounting treatments and does not consider the particular legal or other regulatory requirements of specific countries or jurisdictions.

CONTENTS

MEET THE COACH

Lindsey Byrne is the director of a training and consultancy business started in 2003, working with clients on strategic planning, financial evaluation of business plans and investment appraisal with clients ranging from small businesses to global PLCs.

Lindsey is a CIMA qualified accountant (ACMA) with an MBA from Warwick University, she worked at Marconi plc until 2001 and was part of the team to develop and disseminate their strategy planning process. She also facilitated strategy planning workshops and modelled financial evaluations of strategies and business plans.

Since working as a consultant and trainer, she has assisted many companies with business and financial planning and with the evaluation of accounts and business plans of other companies (potential customers, suppliers and agents).

ACKNOWLEDGEMENTS

Any book on this subject will be the product of the author's exposure to and learning from many business experiences, business managers and entrepreneurs.

Particular thanks must go to:

Glenn Harris MBE for his insight into the best and worst business plans and mistakes he saw when reviewing business plans with a view to awarding funding as part of his role as Deputy Chief Executive in the East Midlands Development Agency.

Neil Johnson, Managing Director of Inviron Ltd, for his insights into the facilities management industry and his inspiring views on how to compete and to make a difference in such a difficult market.

Jason Thorndycraft, Chief Operating Officer of Drake and Morgan Ltd and previously of Novus Leisure Ltd, for his insights into the pub trade and his innovative thoughts on how to seize the opportunities and battle against the many threats facing the industry at the current time.

Nick Byrne, my husband, for his moral support, proof-reading, common-sense checking and good ideas and examples.

And, of course, Nigel Wyatt for getting me started on this project, my publisher Sam Richardson for all his support and Antonia Maxwell, my editor, for her guidance and help.

FOREWORD

It is a universal truism that all businesses, whether they are a fledgling start-up or a multi-national conglomerate, need a good plan.

There are many ways of approaching business planning – many books and consultants too, eager to share their 'miracle template' or insight as though the process were some sort of alchemy.

I can remember my first time ... receiving a glossy business plan summary from my then employer. I was just another face in the finance deptartment then and had no input or involvement in the process. I didn't know much at that stage in my career, but I knew what I was reading didn't resonate with me or my colleagues, nor engaged or galvanized us towards some poorly articulated vision.

I have read and produced many plans since those days, and approved or denied financing to those who have submitted them. What is really sad is when you just know someone has the idea and commitment to succeed, yet hasn't been able to articulate this to extract the necessary finance or support needed.

The key therefore is to provide a clear structure to work around. As in all things, preparation is vital. The work put in at the beginning to define exactly what it is you are aiming to achieve, understanding where you are now, and then plotting the steps, the people and the finances are all needed to be successful.

I have often heard it said, by people much wiser than me, that you learn most by watching somebody who is really talented doing their job well. I have been fortunate to work with, and for, some really gifted people, and have along the way picked up a few tips on business planning that I like to think I still adhere to. One Chief Executive I worked for used to ask if my papers had passed the 'nurse and fireman test'. This meant that if a nurse or fireman just finishing their shift couldn't understand what we had written, then it had failed.

So I have three golden rules:

- Keep it concise.
- Make sure it is understood by all who need to understand it (employees and stakeholders).
- Make progress measurable.

There is a lot of advice and guidance on the subject of business planning. To have a base structure to work with and be clear about what you need to produce a plan is vital. It doesn't give you the answers for your particular business or venture, nor any shortcuts to success. Whether you are new to this, or a seasoned veteran who is seeking affirmation of what you believe a business plan should look like, then there is no better companion to guide you through the process than this book. Good luck!

Glenn Harris MBE

HOW TO USE THIS BOOK

Why bother with a business case? You have a great idea, right? Customers will surely see the benefits in your new product or service, so why do you need a business case?

Whether you're starting up on your own or you're a manager in a business with a great new idea, you need to get other people to back you: with funding, with resources and with support.

Most of us plan for life's changes: moving house, marriage, retirement, etc. Starting a new business venture is no different. You've probably seen lots of benefits to your new idea and thought of many ways to make it work, but what if things don't go according to plan? Nothing in life is certain, but if you fail to plan, it's very likely that the barriers you face will become insurmountable.

Your risk management plans may make the difference between gaining funding and approval or not. One of the first things that banks, business angels and senior managers will look for is your understanding of the risks and how you will manage them. In this book you will identify all the risks, their impacts and their likelihood, but you will also develop plans ready to implement to overcome any difficulties that do arise.

As your business venture grows, you'll need other people to help and support you, whether that's outsourced help, agency or freelance staff, permanent staff members or teams from other departments or business units. Either way, everyone will need to understand what you're trying to achieve. Your business plan will guide others in their day-to-day decisions when you can't be involved in every minute of their time.

Your plan will help you to communicate with those you need to do business with:

- Suppliers
- Customers
- Investors (partners/banks/angels/senior managers/finance department)
- Distributors
- Consultants

How will you convince these people that your venture is credible? You need to look at your business idea from their perspective: what do they need to know to feel you've done your homework? What facts, figures, research, but also what is different about your idea, why should people buy from you, why should others work with you?

Your business plan will form a map to the future that you can review at every stage to ensure you're achieving what you set out to. By reviewing your plan you can spot when the environment changes and alter course accordingly.

This book will help you to produce a business plan whether you are an entrepreneur with a great idea for a new product or service, or a manager in a business looking to propose a new idea; either way you'll put together a convincing business case to win the funding and support you require to take the next steps.

Throughout the book there will be models and ideas to help you plan, activities to complete, including research into your market, as well as templates to fill in to compile your plan. By the end of the book you will have everything you need documented to persuade any stakeholder no matter what their objectives, attitudes or preferred communication styles, to support your new idea.

You'll go through the following steps to ensure your plan covers everything you need to make a success of your new venture:

- Why are you doing this? You'll set out your personal objectives and make sure your business objectives are aligned.

- Who will want your product or service – what is different about you? You'll explore ways of getting the customer to identify your service as the best solution to their needs. You'll also find ways to communicate your values that draw customers and partners to you.

- What's going on in the market? What environmental factors will affect your new venture? What impact will suppliers and competitors have on you? How will you navigate in your new environment?

- How will you organize? You'll find ways to use resources flexibly to grow at the rate demanded by the market without heavy investment from the outset.

- It's a risky business – you'll identify the risks, their likelihood and impact as well as finding ways to overcome them.

- The financials – you'll assess the opportunity to gain backing as well as prepare budgets and cash flow forecasts to help you control your new venture.

- Gaining funding – you'll assess the pros and cons of different sources of funding and how this will affect your control of the business.

- Presenting your plan – you'll establish the needs of all the stakeholders and also their preferred communication styles, to ensure you grab everyone's attention, whether they like 'the grand idea' or the details.

- Implementation – you'll put together detailed operating plans to ensure you succeed in your timescale.

- Reviewing your learning – you'll think about what you have learned this time, to make the next plan even better.

- Determining your exit strategy – how will you grow your business? If you're planning to sell the business at any stage, how will you make it attractive to potential acquirers and how will you value it?

- Finally there is an example business plan, which is laid out as suggested in the book. You can download this and type over it.

Thinking about the future and how your business will grow and thrive, there are shocking statistics for new business failures. According to FinancialPreneur.com 68.9% of VAT-registered businesses cease to trade within ten years of registering for VAT. Not all businesses register for VAT, but of all statistics published in this area, this is probably the most reliable statistic covering business failure.

The leading reasons for business failures found by Mike Pendrith for Performance Point Corporation are:

- No business plan
- Under-funded
- Lack of operating goals and objectives
- Failure to measure goals and objectives
- Failure to pay attention to cash flow
- Failure to understand the industry and the target customer
- No means of differentiation – just another 'me too' business
- Poor or no marketing programmes with which to attract new customers
- Underestimating the competition
- Not cost competitive
- Lack of attention to accounts receivables and inventory
- Poor people management skills

Therefore it makes absolute sense to ensure these are included in the key areas covered in your business plan; you'll find throughout this book advice and templates that ensure you don't fall unknowingly into the same traps as so many others.

Some of the tools included in the book to help you through the business planning process are:

- Coach's tips to draw your attention to a key point
- Coaching sessions enabling you to work through key tasks to realize your own plan

- Online resources including:
    - templates that you can download and complete
    - websites where you can research information to help you compile your plan
- Next steps that review what you have completed during the chapter and that link to the next chapter so you can see where you are in the process
- Takeaways that will get you into a good habit of reviewing at each stage how your business planning is going and what you have learned.

We wish you the very best of luck with your new opportunity.

1 WHY ARE YOU DOING THIS?

✔ OUTCOMES FROM THIS CHAPTER

■ In this chapter we will look at what you want to get out of the business opportunity, to ensure that your personal objectives are taken into account. We'll use these to write the objectives of your business and also to write a mission statement for your opportunity to help you to communicate what the opportunity is about and to get investors, customers, suppliers, partners and potential employees aligned to the vision for the opportunity.

WHY EXAMINE YOUR PERSONAL OBJECTIVES?

The first step is to examine your own personal objectives. For your business idea to be successful, it must fulfil your own personal objectives and align with your needs as well as with the market (and if you're a manager in an existing business, with the company strategy). Make a start by listing and ranking your personal objectives.

Below there are a number of possible reasons why you might want to undertake this venture, to get you started. There is also plenty of space (in Coaching Session 1) to fill in any other objectives you may have.

Step one is to fill in the table with all your objectives and then rank each objective as essential or desirable. If you can establish what is essential to you, then you can set up your business in such a way that it fulfils all these needs. The desirable objectives may still be important, but you may be willing to compromise on some of them. It is very much worth listing them as it will help you to think more creatively about how you could achieve them too. Ranking the desirable objectives out of 10 will help you to prioritize if compromises do need to be made.

Do spend adequate time on this; think it over, sleep on it, discuss it with supportive friends or family members. Only move on from this stage once you are sure that you have listed everything that is important to you. Your business objectives will depend on this; the last thing you want is to build a successful business or grow your business in a way that brings you no personal satisfaction. It will take hard work to achieve your aims, and you will only overcome all the barriers you face if your personal motivation is high.

> **!** **COACH'S TIP**
>
> **Build the business you want**
> Establish your own personal objectives, to ensure the business you build fulfils your needs.

In his book *Delivering Happiness* (see Bibliography) Tony Hsieh says: 'One day I woke up after hitting the snooze button ... six times ... I suddenly realized something ... I was dreading going to work. I was co-founder of LinkExchange, and yet the company was no longer a place I wanted to be.' LinkExchange was later sold to Microsoft and Tony Hsieh then had the opportunity to build another business, Zappos. This time he was able to focus on what was important to him: to ensure the culture of the new company was right. His experience at LinkExchange was a learning opportunity, but you have the opportunity to learn from *his* experience and ensure that you've taken into account all your personal needs and, if you're a manager within an existing business, aligned all your needs with the company strategy before you start and before you find yourself working in a business that you dread going to!

ESTABLISH YOUR OBJECTIVES

Here are some examples of reasons for starting your own business or for proposing your new idea to the board, to get you started:

- Be in control
- Do things the 'right way'
- Launch a product or service you're passionate about
- Escape the rat race
- Gain independence
- Change the world/market
- The challenge
- Grow your business/department
- Gain experience/promotion/be a bigger player
- Have a better work–life balance
- Work with people you like
- Achieve the company strategy
- Gain financial independence/make money
- Build a business and a legacy to pass onto future generations

Make sure you also list all the things you DO NOT want to happen. For example:

- To not work longer hours than currently
- To not start a manufacturing operation
- To not sell directly to individual consumers
- To not lose control or decision making in the business to other investors or lenders

It's important to list the 'must-nots' to ensure that you don't accidentally fall into doing things that you wouldn't want. Partners, investors and employees need to understand fully what your business is about and what it's not about!

Once you've completed this step, step two is to consider all the consequences and business objectives that link with your personal objectives. Here are some examples and some related consequential objectives to help you to get started:

Reason	Consequential Business Objectives/Some things to consider …
To be in control	You probably won't want to take so much external funding that you lose control of the decision making. Will less funding mean slower growth?
	If you are sharing the business opportunity with partners, you need to agree terms for every eventuality (for example, a partner leaving, a new partner joining or how decisions are made).
	Will you want to maintain decision-making control? If so, how will you manage the growth on your own?
To launch a product or service you're passionate about	You will need to make sure others are as passionate. Who are your target customers? Whose support do you need? Do they have similar values and objectives?
To gain experience/a promotion/be a bigger player	Who will help with your existing responsibilities? Do you have a successor lined up? Your management may not support you moving on to work on a new idea if it leaves your existing duties at risk.
	Who else in the company do you need to involve? Who are the stakeholders? What are their objectives? What support do you need from them? How will you convince them to support you?
To gain financial independence/ make money	How much money, over what time frame? If you need to grow very quickly how will you manage that (outsourcing, licensing, franchising)?
	What is your exit plan?
	• Sell the business in five years? In which case you need to consider what will make it attractive: who are the target acquirers and what will interest them? (see Chapter 11 for more on this topic).
	• Grow the business, build a legacy, pass it onto the children? Consider how to grow the business in a sustainable fashion to eliminate the risks, but if this means growing more slowly, how will you defend against bigger competitors taking your idea and taking over your market?

Reason	Consequential Business Objectives/Some things to consider ...
To do things the 'right way'	You will want to set out your values early on and stick to them. Only work with people and companies that will uphold your values. Find a way to communicate your values to customers, suppliers and other stakeholders that will appeal to them and make you their partner of choice.
Have a better work–life balance	When do you want your work–life balance to improve? You might find starting your own business takes up a great deal of your time at least in the short to medium term. You will need to plan carefully and decide how long you're prepared to work hard before you achieve your objectives. Otherwise, you could plan to involve a business manager early on. Will you find this fulfilling? Will you be able to give up control so early on? How much time will you need to invest to steer and direct, especially in the early days?

! COACH'S TIP

What are the consequences of your objectives?

Always consider the implications of the objectives you have identified. What do they mean for how you build your business opportunity?

😀😀 COACHING SESSION 1

Establish your objectives

Now think of your own objectives (and 'must-nots') and list them below. Rank them as essential or desirable. For the desirable objectives, rank them out of 10 and then spend some time thinking about the consequences and business objectives that you need to consider:

Personal objectives/Personal 'must-nots'	Essential / Desirable	Desirable objectives ranked out of 10	Consequential business objectives

→

Personal objectives/Personal 'must-nots'	Essential / Desirable	Desirable objectives ranked out of 10	Consequential business objectives

Personal objectives/Personal 'must-nots'	Essential / Desirable	Desirable objectives ranked out of 10	Consequential business objectives

Personal objectives/Personal 'must-nots'	Essential / Desirable	Desirable objectives ranked out of 10	Consequential business objectives

ONLINE RESOURCE

Personal and business objectives

A downloadable template for your personal and business objectives can be found at:

www.TYCoachbooks.com/Businessplans

COACHING SESSION 2

Imagine your business in the future

Here is an activity to ensure you have considered all your personal objectives: imagine your business (or opportunity) has been up and running for five years. What does it look like? What does it feel like? What is it like to work in? What is it like for employees, customers, suppliers, partners, other stakeholders? How would they describe the business? What have you achieved? What is your typical day like? Make notes in the box below.

This exercise in imagining the future may raise some more ideas to add to your list of personal objectives and consequential business objectives.

YOUR MISSION STATEMENT

You can now use the information you've compiled to write a mission statement. The mission statement is a short statement that you can use to describe your company, its *purpose*, *strategy* and *values* to your investors, existing and potential employees and customers.

> ## ! COACH'S TIP
>
> ### Your mission statement
>
> Your mission statement is your opportunity to communicate your strategy, purpose, objectives and values to all involved stakeholders.

Here are some mission statements of well-known companies:

Apple	To make a contribution to the world by making tools for the mind that advance humankind.
Virgin	We have always succeeded in business by offering consumers another way, a better way and being willing to fight their corner. The world has changed a great deal in the 40 years that we have been in business but we have moved with the times and we have always listened to what people want.
Barclays	We are committed to building a world-class organization. We aspire to be among the most valuable and admired financial services companies in the world: ■ A business that leads in its chosen markets ■ A portfolio of brands that are synonymous with quality and integrity ■ A culture based on high performance and behavioural excellence.
BBC	To be the most creative organization in the world.
BSkyB	We entertain, excite and inspire customers with a great choice of high-quality television in high definition. We make technology simple and put viewers in control.
Rolls Royce	Strive for perfection in everything you do. Take the best that exists and make it better. When it does not exist, design it.
Waitrose	A successful business powered by its people and its principles.

- Which do you find most inspiring? Why?

- Which do you find informative – would they help you to know whether you want to do business with this company?

! COACH'S TIP

Once you've written your mission statement, run it past some supportive friends, family or colleagues. How does it make them feel? Ask them to describe what your company or department would be like to work with based on what they've heard. Does their perception fit with what you intended? Do you need to adjust your mission statement?

COACHING SESSION 3

Reviewing your objectives

Spend a few moments now reviewing your objectives. Try to compile them into a single statement that describes your new business's or opportunity's strategy, purpose and values in an inspiring way that will help:

- existing employees to make decisions when faced with problems outside their normal scope of experience;

- potential employees to identify you as an employer of choice where their values line up with yours;

- customers, suppliers and business partners to understand what your company is about and to want to do business with you.

COMPANY'S (OPPORTUNITY'S) MISSION STATEMENT:

♟♟ NEXT STEPS

In this chapter you have:

- Thought about your own personal objectives and how they fit with your business opportunity.

- Considered the consequences of your objectives, and what this means for how you will build your business.

- Written your mission statement which will enable to you share your strategy, purpose, vision and values to all stakeholders in your business.

In the next chapter you will look at your Unique Selling Proposition (USP) for your opportunity and think about how you will ensure your customers and investors understand what makes your opportunity so irresistible. You'll think about how you are going to differentiate yourself from the competition, and how this might lead to growth in the future.

TAKEAWAYS

This is your opportunity to take stock of what you have learned from this chapter. You might now want to choose other chapters and exercises to focus on, or you can continue to work through the whole book if this better fits your needs.

What objectives did you discover through these activities, that you had not considered before?

Are you confident that you have identified all your personal and business objectives? Who could help you to review them to ensure you have captured everything?

Do you need to go back over anything to clarify your thinking?

What did you learn about writing Mission Statements from reading those of the well-known companies?

Has considering your mission statement made you reappraise your objectives in any way?

WHO WILL WANT YOUR PRODUCT OR SERVICE?

✔ OUTCOMES FROM THIS CHAPTER

- In this chapter we will establish a Unique Selling Proposition (USP) for your opportunity. The aim is to be able to communicate to customers and investors what is so good about your opportunity and product or service. We'll also establish your core competency, to help you to differentiate yourself from the competition – in the future this may help you to grow beyond your current opportunity.

In *Simply Better* Barwise and Meehan (see Bibliography) point out that being the best doesn't necessarily require a unique product or service. It may be that you just deliver on a key customer need really well. How often have you complained to friends about a product or service, but can't be bothered to change providers because the competitors are equally bad? Think about the service you receive from your bank, your mobile phone provider, internet service provider or utilities providers. If one competitor delivered what was really important to you really well, would you buy from them then?

YOUR USP

Think of the last time you met a salesperson, either in your personal or professional life. How did that salesperson describe their company and their products to you? While they were telling you about their company and their product, was everything they said important to you?

Many salespeople will quote their company's or product's 'USP' (unique selling proposition) with little regard to the customer's needs. How often have you heard a salesperson say: 'We have great staff, great products and we strive to partner with our customers to exceed their expectations.'?

This is all very well, but such a generic statement doesn't really add any value to the sales conversation. How often have you sat through a salesperson's presentation, knowing lots of what they're talking about is irrelevant to you, but they seemed to have a speech ready, so you ended up just letting it wash over you?

In a competitive environment, unless you back up your assertions with action, most of these statements are meaningless. But, more than this, if you can tailor your USP to fit with your customes' needs, and personalize all your statements to them, they are more likely to do business with you Later in this session we'll look at how to frame questions to discover our customers' needs and to tailor our sales approach to keep them interested throughout.

However, it's not just about customers' needs and ensuring you have a successful business idea. It's also about convincing those who will support you with resources, funding or moral support that your idea is going to work. You need to be able to articulate what is great about your idea in a way that resonates with all your stakeholders: customers, suppliers, business partners, agents and investors.

Take some time now to list all the things that are good or different about your product or service. Why would people buy from you? What benefits do your product or service bring that the customer can't get elsewhere? Fill all this information into the first column of the table in Coaching Session 4 entitled 'Capabilities – how are they different?'.

We also need to consider *how* these capabilities are different. Alongside each capability, explain how it's different from what the competition can do, but don't use adjectives. 'Bigger, better, brighter, faster' aren't specific enough. For example, imagine you are a finance trainer writing a business plan to set up your own finance training company. You might have said that a capability is being a qualified accountant who has worked as a finance business partner in manufacturing. The differentiation is that your competitors all use experienced (but non-finance specialist) trainers who have picked up 'finance for non-financial managers' as one of their topics without having ever worked in business as an accountant.

The next step is to think of the benefits to the customer of your capabilities. What are all the benefits a customer or any other stakeholder could see in each differentiator?

In our example finance training company, this might be as follows:

- Customers who come to your training courses would learn what is important about each topic to their business and also learn what is important to their finance team – enabling them to learn how to negotiate with the finance department over budget allocations, capital proposals, processes, etc.

- Stakeholders in your business can see that you can provide added value in your courses: perhaps you can charge more, perhaps you will win more business, or perhaps you can target manufacturing companies who will pay for your experience and insight into the industry.

The final columns in the table you are about to complete pose some questions for customers and stakeholders to establish whether each USP is of interest to them, to determine whether to talk about each USP and if so, how to position it.

Going back to our example financial training company, you could ask customers interested in your training courses:

- What do you want to be able to do differently/more effectively as a result of this course?

- Is it important to you that your trainer is a finance expert/qualified accountant/has financial business partnering experience?

- Is it important to you that your trainer understands the manufacturing industry?

Example: financial training company

Capabilities – How are they different?	Benefits – Why would this be important to the customer?	Questions for customers	Points of interest for stakeholders
Qualified accountant who has worked in a manufacturing environment. Other training companies use non-accountants for their finance training.	The customer can learn what is important about each business topic to their business, and to the finance team. They can learn how to negotiate with the finance department over budget allocations, capital proposals, processes, etc.	What do you want to be able to do differently/more effectively as a result of this course? Is it important to you that your trainer is a finance expert? Is it important that your trainer understands the manufacturing industry?	Target manufacturing clients. Charge a premium over generic courses.

Adapted from the DVP from TACK International (see Bibliography)

For more examples, see Chapter 14 which includes a full business plan.

Only if the customer does find these points important is it necessary to explore each point further. If they are not interested, you've saved yourself time but more importantly, you're only focusing on talking about things the customer is interested in and showing real interest in what matters to them.

Additionally, you could talk to other stakeholders (for example those approving your business proposal, lenders, investors, etc.) about your experience in the market, your USP bringing you competitive advantage over existing training companies, and how you will target customers with the needs that you can fulfil.

> ## ! COACH'S TIP
>
> ### Your USP
>
> Your Unique Selling Proposition can be used to communicate with customers to build their interest and desire to buy your offer.

COACHING SESSION 4

Complete the USP definer

Capabilities – How are they different?	Benefits – Why would this be important to the customer?	Questions for customers	Points of interest for stakeholders

—➤

Capabilities – How are they different?	Benefits – Why would this be important to the customer?	Questions for customers	Points of interest for stakeholders

Capabilities – How are they different?	Benefits – Why would this be important to the customer?	Questions for customers	Points of interest for stakeholders

ONLINE RESOURCE

USP definer

A downloadable template for the USP definer is available at:

www.TYCoachbooks.com/Businessplans

CORE COMPETENCIES

All of the work you've done in this chapter is leading to you being able to identify your core competency. A core competency is something that you do differently from other competitors, that customers value and that is difficult for others to replicate.

Your core competency is important to help you to differentiate from other competitors and also to define your market. Consider this example:

If a fertilizer company defines its core competency as 'developing the best fertilizers for lawns' its service will be very different from one which defines its core competency as 'delivering great lawns'.

In the first instance, research and development seems to be what the company values. In this case the company has defined its competency in terms of its own internal strengths.

By redefining its core competency to 'great lawns' it is looking from the customers' viewpoint. What the customer is really interested in is a great lawn. If the company delivers great lawns, it could employ staff to apply the fertilizers, removing the risk of over-fertilization and of killing the grass and takes the hassle out of maintaining the lawn. Crucially, the company also gains the ability to charge more for the service with activities that the customer values.

Your core competency

Communicating your core competency to customers means you can show how you're different from the competition. This will help you grow in the future beyond your current opportunity.

It's important that the core competency cannot be copied by others. What do you think are the core competencies of the following companies?

Coca-Cola	Fizzy drinks manufacturing? Or brand management?
Honda	Efficient cars? Or rate of innovation?
Waitrose	Selling groceries? Or a customer service culture?
First Direct	Banking? Or a customer service culture?

All of these companies have core competencies that are related less to the product and more to some process, method of working or culture. These competencies are far harder for competitors to copy and much easier to apply in different situations or markets to allow the company to grow and diversity.

COACHING SESSION 5

Your core competency

Review the USP definer that you worked on in this section and try to write out your core competency now, in the box below. Remember it should be something that the customer will value and that other competitors would find very difficult to copy.

If you are a manager in business and you're looking to gain approval from senior management or from finance for your new idea, show how your opportunity links with and utilizes your company's existing core competency. Show how utilizing that core competency aids growth and ensures you retain differentiation from the competition.

MY COMPANY'S (OR OPPORTUNITY'S) CORE COMPETENCY:

There is another good reason for knowing what your core competency is. In the future when you are looking to grow the business to a point where you need to diversify, using your core competency to diversify will allow you to grow the business while retaining competitive advantage. Unrelated diversifications (where a company expands into totally new markets, or acquires businesses in different markets) are difficult to manage. How can you be expected to understand a number of unrelated markets and businesses? However, if you can use your core competency in other markets, you can still provide value to customers in these new markets. Consider the following example:

> Enron originally defined itself as a natural gas transmission company, which constrained it to a commodity market where competition tends to be based on price and barriers to entry are lower. Later it redefined its core competency to energy trading. This is where the real skill was in Enron's business. By redefining itself, it was able to use its skills in 'energy trading' to grow rapidly. It was a skill that was transferable to other energy industries thereby expanding the potential market.
>
> Now we've mentioned Enron, you'll be expecting a word of warning. It's important to understand how far to take expansion using core competencies. According to Fusaro and Miller (see Bibliography): 'If Enron had stuck to its core competency of energy trading, this might have worked out well, but Enron ended up making markets in 1,800 different products that spanned dozens of markets.'
>
> Only expand to the extent that your core competency is in place and still providing value to the customer.

→ NEXT STEPS

In this chapter you have:

- Established your Unique Selling Propositions, and explored what their real benefits are to customers. You can use these as a basis to form questions for customers about their needs, so that you communicate with customers only on the aspects of your opportunity that really suit their needs to build their interest and desire to buy.

- Communicated your USPs to your investors to show them how your opportunity is different.

- Established your core competency, so you can communicate how you're different from the competition and also to help you grow in the future beyond your current opportunity. If you're a manager in an existing business, show how your opportunity links to and utilizes existing core competencies to aid growth and further develop differentiation.

In the next chapter you'll be investigating the market in which you'll be trading to see how that will affect how you conduct your business. You'll also think about what threats you might face, and how to take advantage of any opportunities that changes in the future can bring.

TAKEAWAYS

This is your opportunity to take stock of what you have learned from this chapter. You might now want to choose other chapters and exercises to focus on, or you can continue to work through the whole book if this better fits your needs.

Now you've established your USP and looked at the benefits to your customer, how do you feel you know your customer better?

How has establishing your USP given you a strong sense of how you are different from the competition?

What questions will you ask customers to discover their needs and focus your conversations on how you can solve them?

What convincing points do your USPs give you to discuss with investors and other stakeholders?

What are your thoughts on how you might use your core competency as you develop in the future?

WHAT IS THE STATE OF THE MARKET?

✔ OUTCOMES FROM THIS CHAPTER

- In this section we'll be looking at the size of the market, the wider macro-economic environment and how that affects your business, as well as the micro-economic environment in which you'll be trading. Finally we'll put all these issues into a template to determine how to manage your business to overcome any threats and to take advantage of the opportunities that changes in the future can bring.

THE SIZE OF THE MARKET

Firstly, how can you identify the size of the market and how much of that market share is realistic for you to take? Depending on the industry you are entering, you may be able to find some statistics quoted online. Large industries will have many commentators publishing regular updates on industry size, competitors, market shares, current trends in the market.

Commentators will include trade associations and industry institutions, as well as government statistics such as The Office for National Statistics (ONS).

In these same articles you may find information on recent new entrants to the market and their growth. You could use this as a starting point for estimating the amount of market share you could grow over the first few years of trading.

If your company has had other market start-ups in the past, you might be able to use the growth of these as a very rough guide to what is feasible.

! COACH'S TIP

Research

List your competitors and find out their turnover and profit. A good place to start is with their company accounts. If your competitors are large, they may well publish their financial statements on their own website, otherwise you can download a copy of any PLC (Public Limited Company) or LTD (Limited Company) accounts from Companies House for just £1 at: http://wck2.companieshouse.gov.uk//wcframe?name=accessCompanyInfo

When you research the competition, you are trying to find out who their customers are. Their own websites may give you information or again, there may be information in the Chairman's Statement and Directors' Report that form part of their company accounts.

- Do they seem to be growing or shrinking their sales?

- How has their turnover changed over the last few years?

- How has their profit changed?

- Have they been investing in fixed assets?

Fixed assets are things the business owns and means to keep for more than one year (for example buildings, machinery and vehicles, etc.).

If sales have been growing and they have been investing in assets it would appear that they expect the growth to continue. If their sales have grown but they haven't been investing in fixed assets, then how do they expect capacity to keep up with their growth? (For help with understanding the published accounts, review Chapter 7.)

If you have small/medium-sized competitors that operate only in the market you are targeting, it will be easier to look at their accounts as you will be comparing yourself to a similar company. Even larger competitors that have a more diverse offering may have separate legal companies focusing on each market. For example a global conglomerate may serve each market via separate Limited Companies, so you can still access relevant accounts for you to compare to. You can easily find the accounts for each of these separate Limited Companies at Companies House (see later notes in Chapter 5/6). However, even if the competitor you most want to analyse is a single large company focussing on many different markets, do look up their accounts anyway. Many such companies will provide segmentation analysis in the Directors' Report where they split revenues and profits by product, market and or geography. You'll have to look harder for the information you want, but it may well be listed for you.

Once you've found the accounts for your competitors, complete the following to aid your comparisons:

Competitor

Sales growth/decline %	Profit growth/decline %	Fixed asset growth/decline %	Additional information"

We will return to analysing your competitors further in Chapter 7.

WIDER ENVIRONMENTAL IMPACTS

To help you look at wider environmental impacts on your market, use a PESTLE analysis. It will help you to identify all the factors that may have an impact on your business idea right now, in the medium term and in the long term.

You might find that some impacts are difficult to categorize into only one heading. It's not important where you list each impact, as long as the checklist has helped you to think of everything you need to, how you categorize doesn't matter.

PESTLE analysis

You can use a PESTLE analysis to identify wider external impacts for your opportunity now and in the future. PESTLE categorizes threats into political, economic, sociological, technological, legal and ecological.

The table you are going to complete is split into short, medium and long term, to encourage you to identify trends, to imagine what may happen in the future, and to ensure you have plans in place to deal with future issues.

Below is a completed PESTLE analysis of a business plan related to starting up a new public house:

	Now/Short term	Medium term	Long term
Political:	**Threats:** Smoking ban – affects number of customers. Campaigns linking bars to health issues such as obesity, violence and impacts on the NHS.	**Threats:** Potential minimum pricing on alcohol – may affect numbers of customers, tax payable?, money/time customers are willing to spend.	**Threats:** Future potential limits on drinking due to health issues? Potential taxes and 'late night levies'
Economic	**Opportunities and threats:** Economic conditions and living standards – affects money/time customers will spend on entertainment – in good times more, in bad times less.	**Opportunities:** Future campaigns to reduce VAT on restaurants and leisure to fit in with European VAT rates of around 5% to stimulate trade	**Opportunities:** The pub trade is traditionally an employer of young people – with unemployed young people being a target sector for the UK Government, will the impact of current trends on the pub trade be relaxed in future?
Sociological	**Opportunities:** Aging population – cater for different needs of different age groups?	**Opportunities:** Cafe culture? – change product offerings and daytime lighting/theme?	**Opportunities:** Personalization is a key trend with young people – the quality of food and drinks are now a given, perceived entertainment value is a key differentiator, will the ability to mould the experience to make each occasion unique be a future opportunity?
Technological	**Opportunities:** Taking a steer from the airline industry, using technology to improve booking processes?	**Opportunities:** A few pubs and restaurants are using technology to allow customers to order in advance and to order in the bar using different media – for example using their ipads.	**Opportunities:** How might technology be used more extensively in the future to differentiate?
Legal/ Regulatory	**Threats:** Food hygiene regulations – regular inspections? Processed meats scandals – sourcing food supplies. Workplace Pension Schemes adding cost to the business. Licensing laws and difficulties with varying licence agreements.	**Threats:** Greater regulation on food sourcing/labelling – higher cost supplies in the future? An end to cheap pub meals?	**Threats:** Raising the age for drinking to 21?
Ecological	**Threats:** Provenance of products (because of food sourcing scares). Power usage (pressure to reduce carbon footprint).	**Opportunities:** Opportunity to use systems to limit power use? Customers are driving many businesses to sustainable business models. (Marks & Spencer's Plan A is an example of their response to customer demand.)	**Opportunities:** Is there an opportunity to use sustainability initiatives to attract customers? Micro-brewery opportunity?

⊋Ω COACHING SESSION 6

PESTLE analysis

Now complete your own PESTLE analysis for your industry and business opportunity using the following template:

	Now/Short term	Medium term	Long term
Political			
Economic			
Sociological			

	Now/Short term	Medium term	Long term
Technological			
Legal/ Regulatory			
Ecological			

ONLINE RESOURCE

PESTLE analysis

A downloadable PESTLE analysis template is available at:

www.TYCoachbooks.com/Businessplans

YOUR IMMEDIATE COMPETITIVE ENVIRONMENT

You now need to review the impacts of the closer competitive environment. Michael Porter (see Bibliography) suggests the following Five Forces as a good starting checklist to review the competitive environment:

Porter's Five Forces

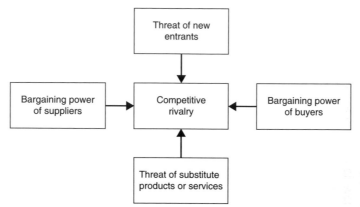

The key to using this model is to firstly describe the situation for your market under each heading, to identify where the situation is beneficial and where it is detrimental for your business, but then most importantly to find ways to maintain any benefits and to overcome any difficulties.

Each force within the model is described in more detail in the table below in the 'description' column. In the 'analysis' column and 'potential response' columns we review the situation for a particular company/industry and potential responses the company could try to improve their situation.

For example, in the technical facilities management (buildings maintenance) industry (also known as hard facilities management) we see a very difficult set of circumstances. Facilities Management companies provide building maintenance services for customers in buildings of any size. The maintenance can be planned preventative maintenance (testing fire alarms, servicing boilers, etc.) or can be reactive maintenance (fixing a leak, replacing light fittings, etc.).

This is a difficult market for many reasons; as you'll see from the table below, most of the five forces we'll focus on conspire to make it difficult to run a profitable business in this industry:

Force	Description	Analysis	Potential response
Threat of new entrants	The ease or difficulty new competitors will find in entering this business to compete with you. The aim is to find 'barriers to entry' to make it difficult for others to steal your market share.	It is very easy for any technically proficient individual to start up a facilities management company, but also easy for companies from close adjacent markets (for example, cleaning or security companies) to look to sell more services to existing customers.	Capital required to start up is very small. There is very little differentiation between service providers in customers' minds. There are few economies of scale – in fact smaller providers are likely to have lower overheads. This is true up to approximately £10–20m of turnover, at which point contracts get to a size where customers tend to require more systems and processes, which are expensive to implement. Only at the £100m of turnover point do businesses start to reap the benefits. Examples of this would be IT reporting systems and mobile engineers. If you have contracts with three or four high street retailers, you can find that mobile engineers can be utilized very efficiently, but if you have only one high street retailer on your books, then having a mobile engineer just incurs lots of travel costs and wasted time between calls. To summarise, while there are no barriers to entry for small firms (for example sole traders) there are clear barriers to growth in terms of capital investment in systems and resources. The only other potential barrier is to focus on how the service feels rather than just on technical proficiency; to build relationships with customers that will lead them to make decisions on quality and service rather than just on price. This means starting small, winning business by displaying a care for the customers' issues, developing relationships rather than trying to win many tenders without any special knowledge of the customer, their industry, their issues, etc., which would no doubt lead to price competition. Once the business is set up, another way to utilize barriers to other competitors entering your market would be to specialize in industries where specific knowledge or licences are required. For example in airports, providers must have airport licences to work airside. Similar situations exist in data centres and rail companies.

Force	Description	Analysis	Potential response
Threat of substitute products or services	Substitute products are not similar products from a competitor, but instead a different product that fulfils the same need. For example the theatre competes with the restaurant as both fulfil entertainment needs.	Two substitutes are: 1. Customers could manage their own facility with internal staff 'in-house'. 2. IT systems that provide computerized diagnostics, known as 'condition-based monitoring' is a current trend to enable monitoring remotely, which enables the manufacturer to build in proprietary monitoring and charge more for the service over the life of the equipment.	1. There is a large portion of the market that is currently self-delivered, but the trend is to outsource, so this is only likely to reduce. The market for facilities management in 2012 is £106.3 billion according to MCi UK Facilities Management Market Research Report 2013. 2. Here the business has to evolve to provide the 'condition-based monitoring' which may be difficult as the manufacturer will protect against losing this valuable income stream, or to gain a 'trusted advisor' position with the client and to advise them at the build stage to consider the full life cost of the equipment over its entire lifecycle to dissuade them from costly contracts. This can be seen as a value added service for customers, who will benefit from advice at this stage and this will help you to build more strategic relationships with customers, making it harder for customers to walk away.
Bargaining power of suppliers	If you have a small number of large suppliers, they will control the market price of supplies and be difficult to negotiate with to attain savings. The aim is to find smaller suppliers, to partner with suppliers or to own your own supply chain to better control costs.	1. Suppliers of components, spare parts, mechanical and electrical equipment, etc. are generally large businesses supplying standard products, so there is little room for negotiation; however this is also a competitive market with many providers, so prices can be quite competitive already. 2. Subcontractors can be of any size, so there is an opportunity to manage subcontract costs.	1. Prompt payment discounts may still be available. 2. The promise of high volumes through 'preferred supplier' agreements may also help with negotiations.

Force	Description	Analysis	Potential response
		3. When taking on a new contract, the kit you must maintain is already in place and manufacturers will try to put in place proprietary systems to monitor and diagnose their kit, so they can provide maintenance and support. Much of new equipment is now manufactured to be thrown away and replaced rather than maintained.	3. There may be potential to win business fitting the new equipment, but again, the equipment manufacturer may sell this service as a package and protect against losing this income stream. As above, advise customers on full life costing of systems at the build stage to add value and develop a more strategic relationship.
Bargaining power of buyers	If you have a small number of large customers, they will control the market prices and it will be difficult to negotiate better rates.	Whilst customers in this market may be of a range of sizes, the service is highly commoditized in the view of the customer. This means that the customer can see no difference between providers (fixing a light fitting is fixing a light fitting – it doesn't matter to the customer how you do it). Differentiation is difficult to achieve and to communicate to customers.	Service excellence and good customer relationships are potentially a way of improving your bargaining power. Added value services (for example reporting systems, partnerships with cleaning and security firms enabling you to share information, work together, share some resources, etc.) may provide a competitive advantage. There is a trend towards 'Total FM' amongst some providers, which means providing all outsourced services. This is difficult to deliver as it's hard to become a specialist in maintenance, cleaning and security and equally hard to communicate this expertise in so many areas to the customer.

Force	Description	Analysis	Potential response
Competitive rivalry	If the product or service is difficult to differentiate, then price competition will be common. The aim is to find a defensible differentiator so that you can charge a price that the customer is prepared to pay for the value you provide.	1. The industry is highly competitive: three year service contracts are common, with customers retendering regularly. 2. Gaining a real understanding of customers needs is difficult, so competition is often price based. 3. When customers award a contract, the existing employees are transferred over to the new provider under TUPE (transfer of undertakings protection of employment regulations 2006) which means that it's very difficult to deliver a very different service from any other provider, as all providers would be using the same staff.	1. As above, service excellence and value added services may differentiate your service. 2. Gaining a real competitive advantage will require a company-wide culture of customer service; this is difficult to engender and maintain in a way meaningful to customers, but if achieved, very difficult for competitors to copy. 3. The only way to differentiate is to implement some kind of change initiative to deliver a very different level of service. Again this would be difficult to achieve, but be very difficult for competitors to copy.

It's important to carry out this analysis when looking to enter an industry, so as part of your business planning, we analyse the situation in order to establish whether this is an attractive industry to join and whether there is scope to compete and to make profits?

It's also important to continually review the model for your industry after you have started up in business. You will want to consider how to use the forces to maintain your profitability, how to discourage others from joining the industry, how to compete effectively by providing something different from the competition, so that you aren't competing on price alone.

! COACH'S TIP

Reviewing the plan

In Chapter 12 we'll look at how to review the whole business plan to keep ahead of the competition.

COACHING SESSION 7

Five Forces analysis

Now compile the Five Forces analysis for your industry:

Force	Analysis	Potential response
Threat of new entrants		

$\longrightarrow$

Force	Analysis	Potential response
Threat of substitute products or services		
Bargaining power of suppliers		
Bargaining power of buyers		
Competitive rivalry		

Porter's Five Forces

A downloadable template for the Five Forces analysis is available at:

www.TYCoachbooks.com/Businessplans

SWOT ANALYSIS

To complete the analysis of the external environment, we need to compile all we've learned in this chapter into the opportunities and threats section of the SWOT (strengths, weaknesses, opportunities and threats) analysis.

When compiling a SWOT analysis, it's important to start with the opportunities and threats and not with the strengths and weaknesses, as strengths and weaknesses are relative to opportunities and threats. A training company could say that a strength is its great trainers, but if we discover the threat that e-learning is destroying the training market, then the great trainers are no longer a strength!

You are going to review the issues you identified in the PESTLE and Five Forces analyses and condense them into opportunities and threats.

COACH'S TIP

Threats and opportunities

Try not to assume that what initially appears to be a threat cannot be turned into an opportunity. If other competitors are suffering from a threat, as a new start-up you may be in an ideal situation to be more flexible and to overcome that threat.

Here's an example of some opportunities and threats for an inventor who has developed a new type of kitchen bin that condenses waste daily, to reduce the amount of times you have to empty it:

Opportunities	Threats
Political: Governments trying to reduce landfill, may be keen to promote your product.	Economic: In times of economic downturn, are people prepared to pay for ecological solutions?
Technological: 'Chip in bin' technology threatens to charge households for non-recycled waste – this would reduce waste and therefore charges.	Sociological: With complaints rising as bins in more and more areas are being collected fortnightly, will residents see this as an unattractive solution?
Ecological: People have a growing interest in ecology, they will be keen to reduce landfill.	Technological: Are there other technological solutions (composting, biodegradable packaging, etc.) that will make your product irrelevant?
Competitive rivalry: No bin manufacturers currently selling this technology for home-owners.	

! COACH'S TIP

SWOT

Another useful tool at your disposal is the SWOT analysis, which examines your business idea in terms of its strengths and weaknesses, and the opportunities and threats that it might face.

COACHING SESSION 8

SWOT analysis

Now start a SWOT analysis for your business opportunity, by considering it in terms of the opportunities on offer and the threats that it might face:

Opportunities	Threats

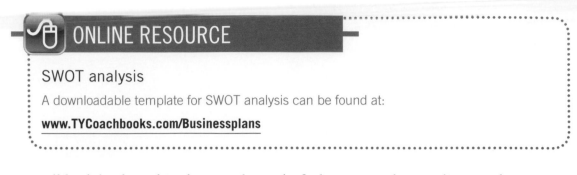

ONLINE RESOURCE

SWOT analysis

A downloadable template for SWOT analysis can be found at:

www.TYCoachbooks.com/Businessplans

We'll look back at this chart at the end of Chapter 5, when we line up the strengths and weaknesses in your internal operations with these opportunities and threats, in order to plan how to take up the opportunities and to overcome the threats.

STARTING A BUSINESS IN AN ECONOMIC DOWNTURN

During an economic downturn may seem like a difficult time to start a new business. In fact, there may be distinct advantages to starting up when economic conditions seem most difficult:

1. Costs may have been driven down during a recession and you may be able to drive a hard bargain with suppliers. Property companies may give longer and longer rent-free periods to attract lessees Potential customers may try to save money too, so they may be more inclined to look at new suppliers, giving you an in-road.

2. There may be a greater pool of unemployed talent willing to change direction and work for a small start-up.

3. Government tax incentives for businesses to drive growth will be favourable in an economic downturn.

4. There may be opportunities to buy second-hand equipment cheaply from other businesses that have fallen on hard times.

5. You'll be focused on being lean – a good philosophy for the future.

6. Competitors will be focusing on their core competencies, their core customers and markets and restricting investment in new opportunities. This gives you a head start on the competition; get into a niche market and grow your presence quickly and larger competitors are unlikely to react until times are better.

Here are some businesses you may be surprised to see started in a recession:

- Microsoft
- Hewlett Packard

- Disney
- GE
- Revlon
- Hyatt
- Federal Express
- Burger King
- CNN

→ NEXT STEPS

In this chapter you have:

- Established the size of your market, using the published accounts of your competitors.

- Established what share of that market is feasible for you to take.

- Used PESTLE analysis to identify the wider external impacts for your opportunity now and in the future.

- Used Porter's Five Forces to establish what is happening in the competitive environment and what actions you need to take to ensure you don't have to compete head on, on price alone.

- Used a SWOT analysis to develop a list of all the opportunities and threats facing your opportunity now and in the future.

In the next chapter you will put together plans for taking up the opportunities and overcoming the threats. You will think about your customers – what is important to them and how can you make your product or service accessible to them.

TAKEAWAYS

This is your opportunity to take stock of what you have learned from this chapter. You might now want to choose other chapters and exercises to focus on, or you can continue to work through the whole book if this better fits your needs.

Now you're really beginning to pick your idea apart, what have you discovered that you weren't aware of?

Which of the models used in this chapter did you find most useful?

Are you surprised at what you learned about your competitors' performance? Which of your plans have you had to rethink in light of this?

What gaps or opportunities did you find to exploit?

Do you have some initial ideas on how to overcome some of the threats you identified?

How do you think you can make the most of opportunities offered by an economic downturn?

4 GETTING YOUR PRODUCT TO YOUR CUSTOMER

✔ OUTCOMES FROM THIS CHAPTER

- In this chapter we will look at how you will market and deliver your product or service. We'll think about what's important to your customers and how you can make it easy for them to find your product or try your service.

MARKETING AND DELIVERY

❗ COACH'S TIP

Your route to market

Your route to market is very important. You may have the best product or service in the world, but if your customers don't know about it, or can't get hold of it, then the best laid business plan will fail.

Imagine a singer/songwriter who has written a really catchy song. Firstly, people need to hear the song, then they need to be able to buy the product. In the past, without a record deal with a music company, marketing the single would have been very difficult. Even if potential customers heard the song and liked it, if enough copies of the CD hadn't been delivered to the shops, the song could never get to no.1 in the charts! Luckily with the advent of the internet, social media and music downloads, a singer/songwriter's route to market is much more straightforward.

Marketing

A common approach to attracting customers is embodied in the acronym AIDA:

Attention: First, you have to get the customer's attention; make them notice your product or service within the bombardment of advertising messages we all see and hear every day.

Interest: Second, you have to get the customer's interest. What is different about your product or service? What are the benefits of using your product or service? What are the advantages of your product or service over those of the competition?

Desire: Third, you have to build a desire in the customer to try the product or service, persuade them that the product or service is right for them; that it will satisfy their needs.

Action: Finally, it has to be really easy for the customer to try the product or service, to spur them into action to actually buy it!

A good starting point is to think about who your customer is:

- Who would want your product or service?

- Why would they buy it?

- Can we use this information to group them together to target how to communicate with them and deliver our product to them?

Review the example below which shows a training professional thinking of starting up a business as a freelance trainer. A trainer working either within a training department in any kind of business, or one working directly for a training company, may want to set out on their own as a freelance trainer. This might be to enjoy more flexibility in terms of what jobs they take on or not, or it might be to create a better work life balance where they can choose not to work away from home, or not to work every day, or it might just be a reaction to redundancy. Any new freelance trainer would need to think about how they attract and retain customers. What type of companies might they want to work for? Why would customers buy from them?

Customer group	Why would they buy?	Attention	Interest	Desire (answer: 'why would they buy?')	Action (make it easy to try)
Training companies	To buy in specialist knowledge to supplement their directly employed trainers.	Identify subject areas missing from their training catalogue. Write a course outline (using their templates/ formats).	Highlight how your course is different from any delivered by their competitors. Why their customers would be attracted.	Research the market for this course. How many delegates might be interested? What additional revenues are available? How does your 'per course' charge compare to a full-time employee?	Allow them to market the course on their website, but only develop the course when bookings are made – so they avoid up-front costs on a risky product.

$\longrightarrow$

Customer group	Why would they buy?	Attention	Interest	Desire (answer: 'why would they buy?')	Action (make it easy to try)
Outsourced HR department providers	To grow their business, providing more services to existing customers	Research their customer base and develop a small range of training course titles that suit their customers specifically		Research typical small company training spend; apply this to their customer base to show the potential revenue opportunity	Partner with them so they introduce you to their customers, but you carry out the sales activity under their branding, then share profits from the courses
All companies requiring training for their staff	To develop employees to fill any skills gaps to achieve company objectives	Research their vision, mission, objectives and values. Link your courses to them to show how you'd add value by helping them achieve their goals		Develop a 'Return on Investment in Training' template to show how your courses help to achieve their objectives and how you'd measure the success	Offer to develop and run a free pilot with a review session to establish the results

COACHING SESSION 9

Your customer profile

Complete your customer profile now using the following template:

Customer group	Why would they buy?	Attention	Interest	Desire (answer: 'why would they buy?')	Action (make it easy to try)

Delivery

What is your route to market? Here are some options to consider, along with their possible benefits and drawbacks:

Market/Channel	Benefit	Drawback
Internal sales team	Control, dedicated team, knowledgeable sales people, good customer contact and information gathering.	Fixed costs of employment, management effort required.
Independent sales force (the Avon Cosmetics model)	Knowledgeable sales people, good customer contact and some information gathering, variable cost of selling – costs only incurred as goods are sold.	Some loss of control of sales team, some difficulty in assuring quality of sales team, their process, knowledge, customer interaction.
Wholesaler or distributor	Reduced costs of distribution, reduced stock holding costs.	Lack of control over sales process, loss of contact with customer (lost opportunities to get customer feedback). Giving away margin that could be retained in your business.
Web sales (own website)	Wide reach, automated process, low cost.	Website development and maintenance, less opportunity to get customer feedback, costly marketing required.
Web sales (through intermediary – e.g. eBay shop, Amazon affiliation, etc.)	Wide reach, automated process, low cost, take advantage of their marketing effort.	Fees/commissions charged reduce your margin.

Market/Channel	Benefit	Drawback
Appointment-making service (cold-calling outsource service)	Removes need for cold-calling, brings in qualified potential customers.	Cost, quality of appointments variable? In other words does the appointment-making service ensure that leads passed on are for the right type of customer, actively considering buying?
Concession in a larger store	Brings customers past your offering.	Cost of renting space, need to ensure good fit of customers (that their customers will be interested in your offering).
Social media	Low cost, easy to manage yourself, could 'go viral' and attract a lot of attention.	Your message may be lost in the plethora of other content, limited scope for of targeting who sees your message.
Ask existing customers for recommendations/word of mouth	Low cost, qualified prospects (your customers will recommend others like them who have similar needs).	Slow growth?
Traditional advertising	High-quality advertising makes a good impression with customers.	Expensive, difficult to target who sees/hears your message.

COACH'S TIP

Mixing your methods

If you use a mix of communication and delivery methods you can ensure the widest possible distribution of your message.

COACHING SESSION 10

Route to market

What routes to market are you considering? Write your ideas in the box below.

Choose a mix of more than one method, to ensure growth doesn't stall if things don't go to plan. For example, your own website will need to be marketed heavily to ensure enough potential customers see it. It will have to compete with other websites and established websites will (at least initially) come up higher on lists displayed by search engines. However if you affiliate your website to Amazon, if you link it to an eBay shop, if you publicize it on social media, if you link it to a relevant video that you launch on YouTube, then all of these actions could help to drive more traffic to your website.

→ NEXT STEPS

In this chapter you have:

- Used AIDA to establish how you will find, attract, group, communicate with, and sell to your customers, making it easy for them to try and to buy.

- Thought about how you will get your product or service to your customer.

- Considered different delivery methods, and the benefits and drawbacks of each.

- Developed a mix of communication and delivery methods for your business with the widest possible distribution.

In the next chapter you are going to think about what resources you need to run your business. You will think about where you will find what you need, and how you will manage it. You will also start to think about funding, and how you might manage with limited up-front investment.

TAKEAWAYS

This is your opportunity to take stock of what you have learned from this chapter. You might now want to choose other chapters and exercises to focus on, or you can continue to work through the whole book if this better fits your needs.

Do you have a clear idea of how to gain your customers' attention, why would they look at your message amongst all the other marketing messages they see every day?

Why do you think your customer will want your product or service?

What would you personally need to make you want to try your product/service out?

How will you physically sell your product or service - are you confident that you have a mix of methods that support each other, making it easy for the customer?

How are you going to track which are the most effective marketing methods?

5 HOW WILL YOU ORGANIZE YOURSELF?

✔ CHAPTER OUTCOMES

- In this chapter we will look at what resources you need to run your business opportunity, how you will source the required resources and how you will manage them over time as your business grows. We'll classify these internal resources into strengths and weaknesses and put them together with the opportunities and threats identified in Chapter 3 to start to put plans together on how to take up the opportunities and how to overcome any threats. We'll also look at some options for starting up with limited investment funding, how you might structure your company and the benefits and drawbacks of each type of structure.

INTERNAL RESOURCES

What internal resources and processes do you need to have in place? How will you source these resources? Will you perform these functions yourself, employ staff to help, use independent providers or agencies or outsource the function to another company?

A key point is to spend money on internal resources where it adds value to the customer. Any other internal functions that the customer does not see, and doesn't provide direct value to the customer, need to be as efficient as possible, or outsourced if they are not business critical.

The acronym QFILMSHOP provides a good checklist to identify resources needed as well as your strengths and weaknesses in each function:

Function	Requirements	How to resource each function
Quality	How will you assure quality of products/services? Is quality a key differentiator for your product or service? If so will you need to spend more time, effort and money assuring quality?	Will you: ● Perform the function yourself? ● Employ staff to help? ● Use independent/ freelance providers? ● Use agencies? ● Outsource to another company?
Finance	What financing do you need? (See Chapters 7 and 8 on financials.) What internal processes are required to control the business? Consider how other companies or internal staff could defraud you. If you were setting out to steal from your business, how would you do it? What processes could stop this happening?	
IT	What systems and controls are required? From the customer's point of view, how easy are you to deal with? Get friends and relatives to test your website and ordering and tell you what was difficult or frustrating. Internally, what management information do you need (for example, budget reports, feedback gathering, etc.)? How will you gather it?	
Logistics	How will you deliver your product or service? Is it costly? Are there alternative options? Review Chapter 4 for getting your product to your customer.	
Marketing	What customer information do you need to collect? How will you communicate with your customers? You will need to welcome and to be prepared for honest and uncomplimentary comments.	
Sales	How will you sell your product or service? Consider as many different methods as possible to ensure that if one fails, there are other channels to back it up. See Chapter 4 for ideas. You'll also want to think about how you collect payments: direct debit, PayPal, etc.	
HR	What people resources will you need? How will you manage them? Will they be employed or independent? How will you ramp up if sales go better than expected? How will you downsize without incurring huge redundancy costs if sales don't go to plan?	

→

Function	Requirements	How to resource each function
Operations	What processes do you need in place to make your product or deliver your service? You'll need to plan the whole operation: how you make the product (in-house or outsourced) or deliver the service (employees or freelance agents), how do you make it scalable it demand takes off, how do you downsize quickly and without excessive costs if demand falls, how do you gather customer feedback, how do you improve your product or service over time?	
Procurement	How will you buy in supplies? What relationships do you need with suppliers? How will they be able to ramp up or down if volume fluctuates?	

COACHING SESSION 11

Internal resources

Fill in the template now, using QFILMSHOP, to describe what internal processes, controls, people resources, etc. you require and identify strengths and weaknesses in each area:

Function	Requirements	How to resource each function
Quality		
Finance		
IT		
Logistics		

Function	Requirements	How to resource each function
Marketing		
Sales		
HR		
Operations		
Procurement		

ONLINE RESOURCE

QFILMSHOP

A downloadable template for the QFILMSHOP table is available from:

www.TYCoachbooks.com/Businessplans

SWOT ANALYSIS

Now let's continue the SWOT analysis you started in Chapter 3 by pulling the information that we've identified above into the SWOT with the opportunities and threats we identified in Chapter 3.

Each function (from QFILMSHOP) can be classified a strength if it will help you:

- to take up an opportunity, or
- to overcome a threat.

Each function can be classified a weakness if:

- it needs to be improved to help you to take up an opportunity, or
- it is causing the threat, or
- it does not help you to overcome a threat.

Opportunities	Threats
Political: Governments trying to reduce landfill, may be keen to promote your product.	Economic: In times of economic downturn, are people prepared to pay for ecological solutions?
Technological: 'Chip and Bin' technology threatens to charge households for non-recycled waste – this invention would reduce waste and therefore charges.	Sociological: With complaints rising as bins in more and more areas are being collected fortnightly will residents see this as an unattractive solution?
Ecological: People have a growing interest in ecology, they will be keen to reduce landfill.	Technological: Are there other technological solutions (composting, biodegradable packaging, etc.) that will make your product irrelevant?
Competitive rivalry: No bin manufacturers currently selling this technology for home-owners.	
Strengths	**Weaknesses**
AIDA: Our link to the Local Government Association (LGA) will help us to spread the word on our new bins as they share the marketing with us making it easy for customers to buy from the LGA website.	I: No control over web sales as using LGA website – may not find out about problems until too late.
Q: Our ISO9000 rating assures customers of our quality product.	M: Only marketing is through LGA, risk of not reaching enough customers.
F: Our flexible loan arrangement with XBank Plc will help us to manage finances however quickly or slowly we grow.	S: Difficult to sell directly to customers, not enough sales people or alternate routes to market.
L: The LGA delivering our bins for us helps with scalable logistics.	H: Limited permanent staff, risks of not being able to scale up if sales are greater than anticipated.
O: Use of many outsourced manufacturers helps with scalability.	

COACHING SESSION 12

SWOT analysis for your opportunity

Now complete the SWOT analysis for your business opportunity:

Opportunities	Threats

Strengths	Weaknesses

ONLINE RESOURCE

SWOT analysis

A downloadable template for your SWOT analysis is available at:

www.TYCoachbooks.com/Businessplans

STRATEGIC OPTIONS

You're now going to review your SWOT analysis which you completed above and list all the options available to you to take up the opportunities, overcome the threats, use your strengths, and overcome your weaknesses. Before you write your list, look at the following example taken again from our inventor's new compacting kitchen bin:

STRATEGIC OPTIONS TO MANAGE SWOTS:

- Arrange a meeting with Department for the Environment to obtain backing and publicity for your product.

- Get Local Governments introducing 'Chip and Bin' to promote your product. Focus marketing efforts on areas with 'Chip and Bin'.

- Conduct a swift and intensive marketing campaign to beat companies such as Brabantia and other potential competitors to market share.

- Get a subsidy from the Department for the Environment, or from LGA, to encourage customers to buy.

- Develop a way to combat any smells: partner with a company such as Febreze for joint marketing?

- Develop Service Level Agreements with LGA to ensure deliveries are not held up if the product takes off.

- Develop Service Level Agreements with manufacturers to ensure no delays to deliveries.

- Develop own website and other marketing efforts to ensure business is not over-reliant on LGA marketing and sales. Include some innovative and cheap social media marketing to ensure marketing is effective but not expensive.

- Develop agreements with temporary staff agencies to overcome scalability issues.

- Partner with complementary product providers to overcome scalability issues.

- Partner with retail organization (eg Tesco) to sell products in store.

COACHING SESSION 13

What are the strategic options for your business?

Now draw up a list of strategic options for your business opportunity:

Strategic options to manage SWOTs:

ONLINE RESOURCE

Strategic options

A downloadable strategic options template is available at:

www.TYCoachbooks.com/Businessplans

COACH'S TIP

Get thinking!

The aim is to generate many options to get the creative process flowing. You don't need to implement all the options, but the more you think of, the more likely you are to identify options that the competition haven't already thought of.

Once you've got a really good long list, you should evaluate each option:

- Is it easy to implement?
- Is it cost effective?
- Is it appealing (to you, to the customer, to the investors)?
- Will it be quick to implement?

Add to your plan all the options that will support your business opportunity.

START UP ON LIMITED INVESTMENT CAPITAL

While this section may seem only relevant to start-ups, actually if you are a manager in a business trying to propose a new opportunity, you may be faced with objections from senior managers around budget constraints. Not all ideas in this section are relevant to existing businesses, however they're worth a quick review to see if any are relevant to your idea.

It's a great idea to start your own business; to have complete control, to do something entirely for yourself, to build something for the future, to pass onto the children or to sell on to fund your retirement, but a major problem with getting started is finding the money! Even if you have some capital available to you, do you really want to risk your entire life savings?

Luckily, there are a number of options to start up with little or no up-front investment needed!

- Buy your company on the internet for a cheap and easy start-up:
    - Companiesmadesimple.com
    - Theformationscompany.com
    - Companyformations247.co.uk
- Get customers to pay you up front for development costs (or on milestones), to keep your cash flow positive.
- Use the resources you already have: work from home, hold meetings at clients' premises or at a hotel or cafe (with free Wi-Fi?)
- Get free advice for start-ups from:
    - Gov.uk/business
    - Britishchambers.co.uk
    - Smallbusiness.co.uk
    - Startupdonut.co.uk
    - Businessadvisorsdirect.co.uk (one hour free consultancy)
    - Is4profit.com
    - Freebusinessforums.co.uk
- Use social media to advertise your business:
    - Twitter
    - Facebook
    - Linked In
    - Upload a short video on a topical issue that will appeal to people. Linked to your website, it will advertise your business and also has the advantage that it can raise your website in search engines like Google.
- Build a website free and host it for free:
    - 1and1.co.uk
    - Moonfruit.co.uk
    - Webs.com
    - 000webhost.com
    - Biz.nf
    - Freehostia.com

- Turn all your costs from fixed to variable: hire temps, lease assets rather than buying them, distribute using a courier/haulage company to only incur costs as you make sales, hire office space as needed from:

  - Regus.co.uk
  - Easyoffices.com
  - Flexioffices.co.uk

! COACH'S TIP

Get started

To start with, keep your 'day job' while you build your business. Work for yourself in the evenings, at weekends or take holidays from work while you build it up. Ask friends, family, etc. to help you to get started, until you're too busy to keep it up and until the cash is starting to flow in.

HOW WILL YOU STRUCTURE YOUR COMPANY?

This section is really only relevant to entrepreneurs starting up their own business. If you're a manager in an existing business, you may want to skip onto the next chapter. There are a number of options available, review the benefits and drawbacks of each before you make your decision:

Legal structure	Benefits	Drawbacks
Sole trader	You can start straightaway, you only need to inform HMRC that you are now self-employed You do not need to publish financial accounts There's no cost of start up	Your liabilities are not limited. If you fail to pay creditors, they can take your personal assets
Partnership	Similar to a sole trader, but working with other people to spread the load You do not need to publish financial accounts for your firm	You will need a partnership agreement to lay out how you will work together, what happens if partners disagree, how you will share profits, etc. Your liabilities are not limited. If you fail to pay creditors, they can take any or all partners, personal assets

Legal structure	Benefits	Drawbacks
Limited company (Ltd)	Limited liability means that creditors have no call on your personal assets, your liability is limited to the amount of start-up capital you invested (which could be as little as £1) There may be tax advantages – consult a tax accountant	The company has to be registered with Companies House (you can buy a company for less than £20 – see the section above) You have to publish annual accounts, so you will incur accountancy fees
Limited liability partnership (LLP)	Similar to a partnership but with all the benefits and drawbacks of a Ltd company	

There are other types of company, for example charities, community interest companies and provident societies, but these are generally run without a profit motive, and so are outside the scope of this book.

→ NEXT STEPS

In this chapter you have:

- Used the QFILMSHOP checklist to work out how to organize your resources internally.

- Finalized your SWOT analysis and used this to generate strategic options for your opportunity.

- Reviewed how to start up with limited investment capital.

- Decided how you will structure your company: sole trader, partnership, limited company or limited liability partnership.

In the next chapter you will look at what risks might threaten your business opportunity. Building this into your planning process is the best way to overcome any issues that threaten to derail you. You will also look to the future also and consider how you will manage risks that may as yet be unknown.

TAKEAWAYS

This is your opportunity to take stock of what you have learned from this chapter. You might now want to choose other chapters and exercises to focus on, or you can continue to work through the whole book if this better fits your needs.

What resources did you identify that you will definitely need?

What flexible, variable cost ways have you found to use those resources?

What key strategic options must you implement?

What strengths, weaknesses, opportunities and threats did you identify that you had not previously?

What ways have you found to start up with limited capital?

What liabilities might you face?

What might influence your decision on whether to form a limited company?

THE RISKS

- In this chapter we'll identify any risks that threaten your business opportunity and how to overcome them. We'll also review how to manage risks and opportunities that occur in the future.

IDENTIFYING RISKS

Any investor or senior manager reviewing your business plan will want to ask about the risks. It is an important way in which they will judge how robust your plans are. You'll also want to identify all the possible risks and put plans in place to overcome them, to ensure that you meet your objectives. The first step is to list all the risks you can think of.

! COACH'S TIP

Brainstorm

It might help to work with a trusted friend or colleague so that you can brainstorm your ideas.

Once you have a list of all the risks, categorize them using the following matrix by how likely they are to occur (probability) and by the impact they will have on the achievement of objectives and on cost:

High	Impact	Low
High **Probability**	Risks categorized as **high probability** and **high impact** are potentially highly detrimental to the business opportunity. Can they be overcome: ● by altering your plans to avoid the risk? ● by insurance? ● by hedging? ● by communicating the issue to all involved parties and ensuring they understand what to do in case the risk occurs? If the risk cannot be avoided, given that it is so likely to occur, will it affect your decision to go ahead with the opportunity?	Risks that are **high probability** but have a **low impact** must still be considered, but are less concerning. ● Can you plan and communicate what to do if the risk occurs? ● You should include in your budget any costs of dealing with the risk (as it is very likely to happen)
Low	Risks that are **less likely** to happen, but still have a **high impact** on the opportunity and/or costs still need to be planned for. Although they are less likely to happen, the high impact means that: ● You should plan how to overcome the risk and put in place triggers that will alert you if the risk is about to occur, so you can put the plans into operation in a timely fashion. ● You should plan what to communicate in case of occurrence and who would need to be involved. Have those communications ready to go, so that everyone is informed and ready to deal with the issue.	Risks that are **unlikely** to happen and would have a very **low impact** cannot be completely ignored, but minimal planning is required.

One key point to bear in mind is that because the matrix forces you to categorize into just four boxes, there is a danger that you may underestimate what is required to manage a risk that you estimate has a 40% probability of occurring and medium impact. How accurate can you be with your estimate of the likelihood? Something you estimate at 40% may be more likely than you think, or changes in the outside environment during the implementation of your plans may change the probability of that risk. Ensure that you treat the matrix as a full grid and plot risks where they actually fall within it (see the example below). Then treat each risk individually and put in place the appropriate plans for that risk; don't blindly choose to ignore a risk in the lower right quadrant based on where it has fallen. Rather, plot the risk within that quadrant where you believe it falls and treat it appropriately for its specific details. For example, Risk 3 below would need a very different approach from Risk 4:

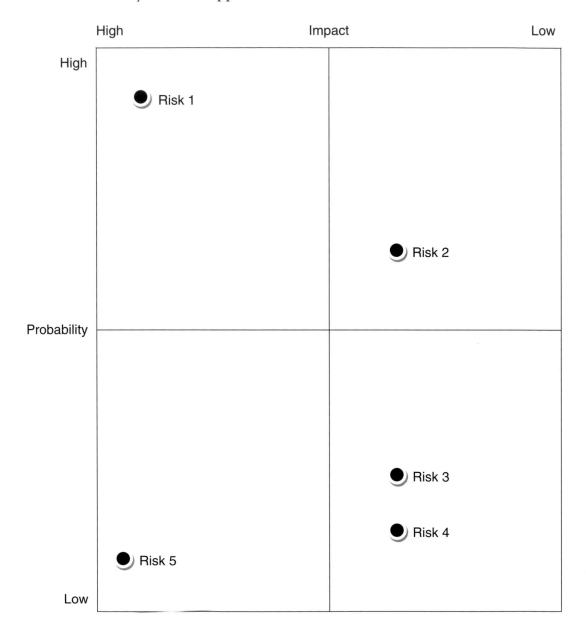

Here are some examples of risks for opening a shop selling organic produce:

High   Impact   Low

High

● Economic downturn

● Few suppliers

                          ● Staff turnover

● Perishable products

● TV programme or report dismissing the benefits of organic produce

Probability

● Trend for organic produce declines   ● Rents and business rates rise

● Inappropriate location   ● Property damage

Low

Risk	Description of risk (what is it, when would it occur, what would be the impact on the opportunity?)	Your mitigation plans to overcome the risk
1.	Economic downturn affects people's spending patterns, people turn away from organic produce	Make it easy to buy, free deliveries, sell items loose in small quantities to reduce waste, offers. Track income weekly, track spend per customer and number of customers to spot trends
2.	Few suppliers drive prices up Competing for supplies with larger retailers (Tesco) drives prices up Track new suppliers as they enter the market	Deal with local suppliers, collect to reduce their distribution costs. Contract for longer periods at fixed prices?
3.	Perishable products	Daily collections of products, sell mixed veg boxes of seasonal/available produce Track sales patterns for each product type Use offers to increase sales of slow-moving stock (buy one fast-moving product, get one slow-moving half price) Give away recipes for veg in season
4.	Staff turnover causes disruption, time to recruit and train on organic knowledge	Recruit locally, staff with a personal commitment to organic/ecology so they are more likely to stay, train on the job, use many part time staff to cover and reduce impact of leavers
5.	Organic trend declines	Hold events in store to promote benefits of organic (for example, cooking lessons, etc.)
6.	Inappropriate location	Careful research required on local demographics and must be close to local organic farmers and distribution links
7.	Rents or business rates increase	Budget carefully, including contingency Negotiate rent free period, contract for fixed rent for a long period
8.	Property damage	Insure

COACHING SESSION 14

Your risk matrix

Complete a risk matrix for your business opportunity now. (In the next coaching session you will go on to describe the risks and your plans for dealing with each.)

	High	Impact	Low
High			
Probability			
Low			

ONLINE RESOURCE

Risk matrix

There is a downloadable risk matrix template available at:

www.TYCoachbooks.com/Businessplans

COACHING SESSION 15

Response to risk

Once you've identified all possible risks and plotted them on the matrix above, complete the table below to describe the risks and your response to each:

Risk	Description of risk (what is it, when would it occur, what would be the impact on the opportunity?)	How to identify the risk	Your mitigation plans to overcome the risk
1.			
2.			
3.			
4.			

Risk	Description of risk (what is it, when would it occur, what would be the impact on the opportunity?)	How to identify the risk	Your mitigation plans to overcome the risk
5.			
6.			
7.			
8.			
9.			
10.			

ONLINE RESOURCE

Risk response table

There is a downloadable template for a risk response table available at:

www.TYCoachbooks.com/Businessplans

MANAGING RISKS AND OPPORTUNITIES

Going forward, collection of information from customers, suppliers, partners, etc. is going to be critical to spot risks and also to identify trends in customer needs, or new opportunities. It would be useful to give everyone working on the opportunity a single form to record ideas, queries, requested changes, etc. from all sources.

The larger your business or project grows and the more people who are involved, the more difficult it becomes to keep track of all the information flowing into the business.

COACH'S TIP

Change control

Generate a 'change control' form and/or an 'information gathering' form either on paper or on your intranet where people can post information as it arises, then have regular meetings to review each point; to understand it, to identify if it can have a positive or negative impact on the business, and how to manage it. This will also engender a feeling of ownership and an ability to make a difference within the whole team.

→ NEXT STEPS

In this chapter you have:

- Brainstormed all the risks to your opportunity and categorized them in terms of probability and impact.

- Considered appropriate actions to overcome each risk.

- Reviewed how you will collect data that flows into the business from different sources, to different employees in different departments.

In the next chapter you will start getting to grips with the finances by looking at the three financial statements that you will need to understand to manage your business. You will look at how to learn from your competition. Understanding your competitors costs will also help you fine-tune your own budgets.

TAKEAWAYS

This is your opportunity to take stock of what you have learned from this chapter. You might now want to choose other chapters and exercises to focus on, or you can continue to work through the whole book if this better fits your needs.

What did you learn about the risks to your opportunity and how they might impact on your business?

What processes do you need to put in place to identify when risks are triggered?

What actions did you come up with to overcome the identified risks?

How will you collect data from the various sources in your business?

UNDERSTANDING THE FINANCIALS

✔ OUTCOMES FROM THIS CHAPTER

- In this chapter you will review the three financial statements that you will need to understand in order to manage your business. You will also use the same statements to gauge the financial health of your business customers (will they be able to pay you?) and suppliers (will they be able to supply into the future?) You will also look at your competitors to help you understand their costs, double-check your budgets, and to benchmark-what do they do well and think about what you can do better or differently.

FINANCIAL STATEMENTS

The financial statements consist of three main documents; the Profit and Loss Account (also known as the Income Statement, the Statement of Profit and Loss, The Income and Expenditure Statement and in the USA the Statement of Operations), the Balance Sheet (also known as the Statement of Financial Position) and the Cash Flow Statement. You will need to understand these documents and what they can tell you about a business for the following reasons:

- **For competitor analysis**: to enable you to estimate your likely profits before starting up.

- **For customer analysis**: will they be able to pay you?

- **For supplier analysis**: are they a stable, sustainable business? Will they be able to continue to supply you in the long term?

- **To manage your business**: to understand your company performance, solvency, liquidity and risk.

- **To communicate with your senior managers or investors**: to assure them of the safety of their investment and the performance of your business.

- If you intend to start up a limited company you will be required to publish annual accounts.

- If you intend to start up as a sole trader, while you will not be required to publish your financial statements, you will still need to produce at least a Profit and Loss Account in order to complete your tax returns.

THE PROFIT AND LOSS ACCOUNT

The Profit and Loss Account shows all the day-to-day income and expenditure of a business for a period of time, usually 12 months, although the first accounting period may be shorter or longer than a year to fit into your desired accounting year end.

Here is an example Profit and Loss Account:

Profit and Loss Account for ABC Company Ltd for the year ended 31/12/2013

	Note	£
Revenue	1	1,000,000
Cost of Sales	2	(400,000)
Gross Profit	3	**600,000**
Overheads		
Admin and management salaries	4	(100,000)
Rent and rates		(100,000)
Utilities		(100,000)
EBITDA	5	**300,000**
Depreciation and amortization	6	(100,000)
Operating profit (EBIT)	7	**200,000**
Interest	8	(20,000)
Profit before tax		**180,000**
Tax	9	(70,000)
Net profit	10	**110,000**
Proposed dividend		(60,000)
Retained profits	11	**50,000**

COACH'S TIP

Ask the experts

Take advice from a qualified tax accountant when deciding on your year-end date, as there may be tax advantages to a short or long first accounting period.

Notes

1. Revenue is recognized (counted in the Profit and Loss Account) when the goods or services are delivered, not when the cash is received from the customer.

   The only complication to this is if you are working on a long-term contract. Imagine a situation where you have contracted to work on a three-month project for a customer.

You probably won't want to wait until your work is complete to invoice the customer. In this instance, you can agree with the customer that they pay you on certain milestones. These milestones may be discrete elements of the contract (for example you may invoice when the design is complete, then again when the design is tested, then finally when the solution is implemented) or may be on the basis of hours spent (in which case you could invoice monthly). In this case revenue would be recognized as invoices are raised.

2. The Profit and Loss Account is produced on the 'accruals basis' which means that we account for the costs that match with these revenues, i.e. just the costs of the goods sold, not all the stock bought.

   Cost of sales is the costs purely associated with the provision of goods or services. For a retail outlet, just the costs of goods bought in and sold on, for a manufacturer this would be the costs of components and the labour cost associated with assembly of the goods, but not the costs of management or supervision.

3. Gross profit is the profit made on the sales of goods or services; at this stage no overheads have been accounted for.

   Gross margin is gross profit expressed as a percentage of sales revenue (in the example 60%).

4. Overheads are costs that do not touch the product or service. They are accounted for on the accruals basis when the cost is incurred. So for example if your utilities are billed quarterly, you must account for the estimated costs in each of the months. Suppose you expect a telephone bill for £150 per quarter, you will accrue (or estimate) £50 for each month until the bill is received; at that stage you would correct any errors in your estimates. So in April you accrue £50, in May you accrue £50 then when the bill arrives in June for £170, you would account for the £70 not yet accrued for in June's accounts.

5. EBITDA (earnings before interest, tax, depreciation and amortization) is a profit level that is not required to be published in accounts. However, it is useful for valuing a business. (We will return to this topic in Chapter 13.)

6. Depreciation is the spreading of the cost of a fixed asset over its useful life. If you bought a car that you intended to use for three years, you would spread the cost of the car over three years. Depreciation is part of the accruals concept. Account for the cost of the car as you use it. See the following example:

Accounting Year	Cost	Depreciation	Net Book Value
1	£12,000	£4,000	£8,000
2		£4,000	£4,000
3		£4,000	£0

The cost of the car (assuming it was paid for in cash) would be accounted for in the Cash Flow Statement immediately after that the cash was paid out.

The depreciation would be accounted for in the Profit and Loss Account in order to spread the cost fairly in relation to the use of the car.

The Net Book Value is the value expressed in the Balance Sheet at year end.

Amortization is the writing down of an intangible asset. An intangible asset is something the business owns (and means to keep for more than one year) but unlike buildings and machinery, can't be touched. For example if the business bought a patent, or a licence, a brand, or software. Under UK GAAP (the rules that UK limited companies have to apply in publishing their accounts) goodwill is amortized. Goodwill is the price paid to acquire a company less the net asset value of that company. It's the excess paid over the asset value, based on what the acquirer is willing to pay for the future cash flows of the business. When someone sells a business, they are giving up the assets, but also giving up the income stream. They want to be compensated for the sale of the assets and also for losing their income. When two parties negotiate an acquisition, the value of future cash flows will be forecasted and the value of them negotiated to establish the purchase price.

When the acquisition is completed, the goodwill has to be valued for the Balance Sheet. Consider this example: You buy my business for £1m. My business has assets of £50k (equipment, vehicles and fixtures and fittings). When you add my Balance Sheet into yours, your cash has reduced by £1m. Your assets have increased by £50k. Your Balance Sheet doesn't balance any more. You must add the difference between the price you paid – £1m and the net asset value – £50k into your fixed assets as goodwill: £950k.

Under UK GAAP this goodwill can be amortized. The amortization calculation is the same as depreciation, the only difference is the terminology; we depreciate tangible fixed assets and amortize intangibles.

US companies, under US GAAP, do not amortize goodwill, instead they regularly test the goodwill for impairment. (If the company acquired is no longer worth what was paid, the goodwill is written down [impaired] in the balance sheet by the loss in value. This is also accounted for in the statement of operations [profit and loss account] as a cost.)

7. Operating profit (also known as EBIT – earnings before interest and tax) is the profit after all business running costs).

   Operating margin is operating profit expressed as a percentage of sales revenue.

8. Interest is the net of interest paid and interest received.

9. Tax is the corporation tax due on profits. You are strongly advised to consult a tax accountant to help with ensuring you are taking advantage of all tax efficient ways of working.

10. Net profit is the profit attributable to shareholders. From this the owners of the business can decide to take dividends, or instead choose to leave the profits in the business to fund future growth.

    Net margin is net profit expressed as a percentage of sales revenue.

11. Retained profit is the amount of profits left in the business to fund future growth. This figure is shown on the Balance Sheet in Reserves. See the next section on the Balance Sheet (note 11) for more information.

THE BALANCE SHEET

The Balance Sheet (or Statement of Financial Position) shows a statement (or snapshot) at the year end of everything the business owns (Assets) and everything the business owes (Liabilities and Capital).

Below is an example Balance Sheet.

Balance Sheet for ABC Company Ltd for the year ended 31/12:

	Notes	2013 £	2013 £	2012 £	2012 £
Fixed Assets (Non-Current Assets)					
Property, plant and equipment	1		300,000		200,000
Investments	2		100,000		100,000
Goodwill	3		100,000		150,000
Total Fixed Assets			**500,000**		**450,000**
Current Assets					
Stock (Inventory)	4	15,000		10,000	
Debtors (Accounts Receivable)		10,000		17,000	
Cash		0		100,000	
Total Current Assets		**25,000**		**127,000**	
Creditors: Amounts falling due within 1 year (Current Liabilities)					
Tax due	5	(70,000)		(50,000)	
Creditors	6	(20,000)		(25,000)	
Dividends proposed		(60,000)		(50,000)	
Overdraft		(5,000)		0	
Total Current Liabilities		**(155,000)**		**(125,000)**	
Net Current Assets	7		**(130,000)**		**2,000**
Creditors: Amounts falling due after more than 1 year (Non-Current Liabilities)					
Long term loan (borrowings)	8		(70,000)		(202,000)
Net Assets	9		**300,000**		**250,000**
Shareholder Funds (Equity)					
Called Up Share Capital	10		150,000		150,000
Profit and Loss Account Reserves	11		150,000		100,000
Total Shareholder Funds (Total Equity)	12		**300,000**		**250,000**

! COACH'S TIP

Balance Sheet formats

The Balance Sheet shown here is in the format used by limited companies under UK GAAP (United Kingdom Generally Accepted Accounting Practices). There are alternative formats available to PLCs under IFRS (International Financial Reporting Standards), and for Incorporated Companies under US GAAP. For the purposes of this text, it is mainly the formats and terminology that are different under the different sets of standards. (Alternative terminologies are listed in brackets after each item where there is a difference.)

Notes

1. Fixed assets are things the company owns and intends to keep for more than one year. Examples would be land, buildings, machines, vehicles, office equipment, etc.

2. Investments are shares owned in another business.

3. Goodwill is only seen on the Balance Sheet if the company has acquired another. Goodwill is the difference between the price paid to acquire a company and that company's net asset value. When acquiring a business you will have to pay for the assets bought but also for the future cash flows (this is the income that the vendor is giving up when selling their business). On acquisition, you will add the value of bought assets into your Balance Sheet, the cash value in your Balance Sheet will fall by the cost of the acquisition, but if you paid £100k for a business which was split between total assets of £30k and £70k of forecasted future cash flows, the Balance Sheet would be out of balance by £70k. This is represented by the goodwill which is placed into the fixed assets to bring the balance sheet back into balance. In Chapter 13 we will be looking at your 'exit strategy' and discussing how to value your business and therefore how to value goodwill.

4. Current assets are things the company owns but will turn over within a year. Examples are stock, debtors (customers who owe us money) and cash.

5. Current liabilities are things the company owes but will need to be paid within a year. Examples are creditors (suppliers who we owe money to), etc.

6. Creditors are suppliers that the business owes money to. Supplies have been received, the invoice has been received but not yet paid for. There may also be accruals listed in this section, this is where supplies have been received but the value is estimated as the invoice has not yet been received.

7. The Net Current Assets figure has been calculated in a separate column for the sake of clarity for this example. As you can see, only the Net Current Assets figure has been added to the Fixed Assets in the total column. Net Current Assets is also known as Working Capital. This is the difference between current assets and current liabilities. In this example Balance Sheet it's actually a net current liability in 2013 as liabilities exceed assets. This is an important figure as it gives a clue to the liquidity of the company. This figure shows whether the company has enough cash (or cash due in from customers or stock that could be sold) to pay the bills due right now. In this instance in 2013 the

company does not have enough cash to pay the bills and this shows us there may be a liquidity problem. Depending on the type of business, this may be a problem or maybe not.

For example, if this were Tesco's Balance Sheet, there would be no problem. Tesco generates cash every day and so if they do not have enough cash to pay the bills today, they will tomorrow. Furthermore, you could not imagine Tesco's creditors joining together to force Tesco into liquidation!

As another example, if this were a Balance Sheet for a company like Amazon, this would reflect a very clever business model where there is little or no stock (with books on sale or return), little or no debtors (customers pay by credit card on ordering) and cash is re-invested in the business very efficiently, leading to very low current assets. However, such a business might pay its creditors relatively slowly, so whilst the working capital figure is negative, this shows a business using creditors' money to fund their business cycle. Again, there would be no concern over their ability to pay creditors as the business generates lots of cash every day.

As a further example, if a manufacturing business had negative working capital, it is likely that this would reflect a liquidity problem and supplying such a company might mean slow payments or potentially bad debts.

8. Long-term liabilities are what the business owes and will pay after more than one year. This could include long-term loans (the capital value of the loan only – the interest paid each month is reflected in the Profit and Loss Account), tax due after more than one year, etc.

9. Net Assets is the sum of total assets less total liabilities. You can think of this as, very roughly, if the business closed down, sold all its assets and paid of all its liabilities this would be the cash value left over. This is only a rough figure as assets and liabilities on the Balance Sheet may not be valued at the true market value. For example the fixed assets will have been depreciated through the Profit and Loss Account, but buildings may have increased in value in the real world. If values of assets on the Balance Sheet are significantly overvalued compared to true market values, they would have to be written down (impaired) to the fair value (market value). However, assets are not 'written up' if they increase in value. There is an exception to this in that property (buildings) only may be re-valued to the fair (market) value; however this is not the preferred accounting treatment, so generally they will be stated at original cost less accumulated depreciation the same as all other assets. See the note on depreciation under the section on Profit and Loss Accounts note 6.

The Net Asset value is also an important figure to look out for. If this were negative, then by definition the equity will also be negative. This is a very strong indication that the business is insolvent. The true definition of insolvency according to the UK Insolvency Act 1986 is when a company is "deemed unable to pay its debts". If the Net Assets figure were negative or very small, it would suggest that when any debts fall due, the company would be unable to pay them, even by selling assets. To test for sure, check the loans on the Balance Sheet, read the notes to discover when the loan falls due, look at the Cash Flow Statement to see how much free cash is generated each year and make a judgement as to whether the business can afford to pay its debts.

10. Called-up share capital is money paid into the business by the owners in buying shares either at start up or since to fund growth.

11. Profit and Loss Account Reserves are an accumulation of all the net profits retained in the business (i.e. not paid out to shareholders as dividends) since the business started. Make no mistake, this is not real cash. It merely states where the money came from. It may have been spent on assets. Remember, the true cash figure is listed in the current assets.

12. Total Equity is the total investment by shareholders (from their original capital invested plus profits they chose to leave in the business to fund future growth [reserves]).

ANALYSING THE ACCOUNTS

Now that we've looked at the Profit and Loss Account and the Balance Sheet we can start to analyse the performance of the business.

In order to do this we first must look at the big picture and determine what we expect to see in the accounts of the business to be analysed, so that we know what kinds of ratios we expect to see. To do this we will perform SCIRE analysis (sector, company, information available, ratios and evaluation):

Section	Questions to ask/information to find	Analysis of the situation
Sector To start with, simply brainstorm everything that you know about the industry; ask people who might know about the industry and do some internet research.	Is it growing or is it in decline?	If the industry is growing, providers may be able to charge higher prices; at least they're unlikely to be in direct price competition, so gross margins may be higher.
	Is it very competitive with many commodity providers or is it very differentiated?	In a commodity market, price competition will be fierce, leading to lower margins.
	Is there much consolidation in the industry (companies acquiring each other)?	If there is a lot of consolidation, maybe there is over capacity in the market which may adversely affect margins. Also, with many acquisitions, investments will be high, any return on investment ratios may be depressed.

→

Section	Questions to ask/information to find	Analysis of the situation
	What is the business model (where are most of the costs in the industry – in cost of sales or in overheads?	If more of the cost is in cost of sales it will be important to the competitors to keep prices high and maintain margins. If overheads are high and cost of sales low, competitors will be keen to discount to gain more customers, to cover the overheads.
	Have there been any one-off events affecting the industry?	Any events, such as an ash cloud, a terrorist event, or a major change in price in a key raw material will affect margins.
Company To start with, simply brainstorm everything that you know about the company, ask people who might know and do some internet research.	Is the business a high-end provider with a differentiated product or 'pile them high sell them cheap'?	This will have a big impact on the margins.
	Are they an innovative company launching new products?	If so, there will be high investments in R&D (research and development). How are they funding this? Is gearing high? Gearing is the extent to which a company is funded by loans compared to equity. If gearing is high (a high level of loans) this is risky as there will be a high cost of interest to bear.
	What kind of assets does this company hold?	If high fixed assets are required, where did they get the funding? Is gearing high? Is a lack of capital constraining their growth? If high stocks, how is this affecting their cash management and liquidity ratios?
	Is the business growing or in decline?	If growing, how are they funding this? Is gearing high? Are there high investments in marketing and capital investments? These in the short term will reduce the operating margin and ROI (return on investment) ratios.

Section	Questions to ask/information to find	Analysis of the situation
Information available Read the Chairman's Statement and Directors' Reports, look at the business's website	Review the company strategy and commentary about the market; does it line up with what you thought in the previous two sections?	
Ratios	See next section for a thorough exploration of ratios.	
Evaluate	Once you've completed all the ratios, compile all the information you've gathered and determine: ● Is the company doing the right things given the state of the market? ● Do the ratios fit with your estimates? ● How does each company compare to its competitors? ● Do the written statements and ratios line up?	

Remember, you're conducting this analysis on:

- Customers – to make sure they can pay

- Suppliers – to make sure they will be around in the future to supply you

- Competitors – to establish the state of the market and whether it is an attractive proposition for you to enter the market, and to benchmark against their costs as a double-check for your budgeting and to establish how you can manage your business in a different way or in a more cost effective way.

COACHING SESSION 16

Your SCIRE analysis

Start your SCIRE analysis now with the SCI sections:

Section	Questions to ask/ information to find	Analysis of the situation
Sector To start with, simply brainstorm everything that you know about the industry; ask people who might know about the industry and do some internet research.	Is it growing or is it in decline?	

Section	Questions to ask/ information to find	Analysis of the situation
	Is it very competitive with many commodity providers or is it very differentiated?	
	Is there much consolidation in the industry (companies acquiring each other)?	
	What is the business model (where are most of the costs in the industry – in cost of sales or in overheads?)	
	Have there been any one-off events affecting the industry?	
	Is the business growing or in decline?	
Company To start with, simply brainstorm everything that you know about the company; ask people who might know and do some internet research.	Is the business a high-end provider with a differentiated product or "pile them high sell them cheap"?	

→

Section	Questions to ask/ information to find	Analysis of the situation
	Are they an innovative company launching new products?	
	What kind of assets does this company hold?	
Information available Chairman's Statement and Directors' Reports, website	Review the company strategy and market commentary; does it line up with what you thought in the previous two sections?	

ONLINE RESOURCE

SCIRE analysis template

A downloadable SCIRE analysis template is available at:

www.TYCoachbooks.com/Businessplans

RATIOS

Ratios are a really useful way of comparing financial results of different companies.

COACH'S TIP

Comparing like with like

The companies you want to analyse will be different sizes with different turnover and different levels of investment. By calculating ratios, you can compare like with like.

We will look at a number of different ratios:

- Profitability on sales
    - How profitable are the companies you are evaluating?
    - How much money do they make on selling goods?
    - What do they spend on running the business (the overheads)?
    - What net profit do they make after all costs?
- Return on Investment
    - What profits do they make as a percentage of the investment made?
- Measures of efficiency
    - How well do they manage their working capital and therefore their cash?

! COACH'S TIP

Poor cash management

Poor cash management is one of the biggest reasons for business failure. A review of how much other businesses in the industry invest in working capital and how they manage their cash flow will be helpful for you to establish your working capital needs. In many industries credit terms with customers are fairly standard across the industry, the same is true of credit terms with suppliers. In addition, most businesses in the industry will have similar stock holdings in terms of days. They will all be trying to manage their stock as efficiently as they can. So you will be able to use their ratios to plan your stock holding needs.

- Liquidity ratios

    - How well do competitors in this industry manage their cash flow?

    - Is cash tight? Do they have enough cash to pay creditors on time? If not, you will need to ensure you have suitable overdraft facilities to cover this. You will also need to negotiate with your bank and keep them informed, showing them how you manage your cash as effectively as possible so that they don't get any nasty surprises in terms of your overdraft requirements and decide to withdraw the overdraft facility!

- Risk ratios

    - The gearing ratio will show you how much other businesses in the industry had to borrow (compared to money invested by the owners) to start up, run and grow their businesses. The greater the gearing percentage (i.e. the more borrowed compared to owners' investments) the higher interest rates are likely to be. As a rough guide a 30% gearing is seen as quite reasonable but anything much higher than 30% could lead to high interest rates and difficulties in gaining more loan funding.

Ratio	Calculation	Comments
Profitability on sales		
Gross margin	$\dfrac{\text{gross profit}}{\text{annual sales}} \times 100$	Profit made on selling goods or services before overheads are paid. Needs to be compared to competitors to determine if GM% is good.
Expenses	$\dfrac{\text{expenses}}{\text{annual sales}} \times 100$	If a company is growing its sales, its fixed overheads should stay relatively stable, so the ratio should go down. If a company is in decline you'd look for them to take action to reduce overheads and keep the ratio stable.

Ratio	Calculation	Comments
Net profit margin	$\dfrac{\text{net profit}}{\text{annual sales}} \times 100$	Comparison to competitors is required to determine whether the ratio is good.
Return on Investment		
Return on Capital Employed (ROCE)	$\dfrac{\text{net profit}}{\text{total equity plus long term loans}} \times 100$	Must satisfy shareholders requirements for a return on their investment.
Measures of efficiency		
Stock days	$\dfrac{\text{stock}}{\text{cost of sales}} \times 365$	The average number of days that stock is held for. Shorter is more efficient; ties up less cash. If stock days are long, check the liquidity, i.e. the current or quick ratio.
Debtor days	$\dfrac{\text{debtors}}{\text{sales revenue}} \times 365$	Average number of days it takes to collect cash from customers.
Creditor days	$\dfrac{\text{creditors}}{\text{cost of sales}} \times 365$	Average number of days it takes to pay suppliers.
Liquidity ratios		
Current ratio	$\dfrac{\text{current assets}}{\text{current liabilities}}$	A ratio of 1 or more is good, as it means the company can pay all its bills. Take into account the business model. If the business generates lots of cash the current ratio could be lower than 1 and still be viable.
Quick ratio	$\dfrac{\text{current assets} - \text{stock}}{\text{current liabilities}}$	If stock days are long, it's not realistic to include stock in the current assets, it would take too long to sell them and get the cash in to pay the bills that are due now. The solution to this ratio, as with the current ratio should be 1 or more.
Risk		
Gearing	$\dfrac{\text{long-term loans}}{\text{total equity plus long-term loans}} \times 100$	Gearing is a measure of risk. A company 100% funded by debt is risky as it will have to pay a high fixed cost of interest; any small drop in sales and profits will make it difficult to pay the interest. However, some gearing is desirable to leverage the owners' investment. Around 30% gearing is usually seen as reasonable by banks. Greater gearing will probably lead to higher interest rates being charged by banks.

! COACH'S TIP

Coach's tip

You only need to calculate either Current Ratio or Quick Ratio. If the stock holding days are long, it's not appropriate to assume that you can use stock to sell to raise cash to pay bills - it will take too long. So in this case use the Quick Ratio.

If stock turns over very quickly, then it can be turned into cash quickly to pay the suppliers. In this case use the Current Ratio. For example, when reviewing Tesco, calculate the Current Ratio. When reviewing a Christmas tree growing company (who only sell stock once per year) calculate the Quick Ratio.

Here is an example to show how the calculations work, using ABC Company Ltd from above:

Ratio	Calculation	Calculation	Result
Profitability on sales			
Gross margin	$\dfrac{\text{gross profit}}{\text{annual sales}} \times 100$	$\dfrac{600,000}{1,000,000} \times 100$	60%
Expenses	$\dfrac{\text{expenses}}{\text{annual sales}} \times 100$	$\dfrac{400,000}{1,000,000} \times 100$	40%
Net profit margin	$\dfrac{\text{net profit}}{\text{annual sales}} \times 100$	$\dfrac{110,000}{1,000,000} \times 100$	11%
Return on Investment			
Return on Capital Employed (ROCE)	$\dfrac{\text{net profit}}{\text{total equity plus long term loans}} \times 100$	$\dfrac{110,000}{(300,000 + 70,000)} \times 100$	29.7%
Measures of Efficiency			
Stock days	$\dfrac{\text{stock}}{\text{cost of sales}} \times 365$	$\dfrac{15,000}{400,000} \times 365$	13.7 days
Debtor days	$\dfrac{\text{debtor profit}}{\text{sales revenue}} \times 365$	$\dfrac{10,000}{1,000,000} \times 365$	3.7 days
Creditor days	$\dfrac{\text{creditors}}{\text{cost of sales}} \times 365$	$\dfrac{20,000}{400,000} \times 365$	18.3 days

$\longrightarrow$

Ratio	Calculation	Calculation	Result
Liquidity ratios			
Current ratio	$\dfrac{\text{current assets}}{\text{current liabilities}}$	$\dfrac{25{,}000}{155{,}000}$	0.16
Quick ratio	$\dfrac{\text{current assets} - \text{stock}}{\text{current liabilities}}$	$\dfrac{10{,}000}{155{,}000}$	0.06
Risk			
Gearing	$\dfrac{\text{long-term loans}}{\text{total equity plus long term loans}} \times 100$	$\dfrac{70{,}000}{(70{,}000 + 300{,}000)} \times 100$	18.9%

○○ COACHING SESSION 17

Calculating ratios for your competitor

Calculate the ratios for a competitor now (it's good to compare two years, in order to see if things are improving or not).

If you can find any additional information that would help you to get an idea of specific costs, calculate each cost type as a percentage of sales – for example: advertising, royalties, product development, etc.

Ratio	Calculation	Current year	Comparison previous year
Profitability on sales			
Gross margin	$\dfrac{\text{gross profit}}{\text{annual sales}} \times 100$		
Expenses	$\dfrac{\text{expenses}}{\text{annual sales}} \times 100$		
Net profit margin	$\dfrac{\text{net profit}}{\text{annual sales}} \times 100$		
Return on Investment			
Return on Capital Employed (ROCE)	$\dfrac{\text{net profit}}{\text{total equity plus long-term loans}} \times 100$		

Measures of efficiency			
Stock days	$\dfrac{\text{stock}}{\text{cost of sales}} \times 365$		
Debtor days	$\dfrac{\text{debtors}}{\text{sales revenue}} \times 365$		
Creditor days	$\dfrac{\text{creditors}}{\text{cost of sales}} \times 365$		
Liquidity ratios			
Current ratio	$\dfrac{\text{current assets}}{\text{current liabilities}}$		
Quick ratio	$\dfrac{\text{current assets} - \text{stock}}{\text{current liabilities}}$		
Risk			
Gearing	$\dfrac{\text{long-term loans}}{\text{total equity plus long-term loans}} \times 100$		
Additional useful ratios			

ONLINE RESOURCE

Ratios template

A downloadable ratios template in excel that will complete the calculations for you as you enter the figures from the financial statements is available at:

www.TYCoachbooks.com/Businessplans

COACHING SESSION 18

SCIRE analysis: evaluation

Now complete the final stage of your SCIRE analysis with the overall evaluation. What have you learned about your competitors?:

Section	Questions to ask/ information to find	Analysis of the situation
Evaluation Put together all the information gathered in the previous sections	What did you determine about the industry and the competitor?	
	What did you discover about the competitor from the written statements supporting the published accounts and from your web search?	
	Did the ratios line up with what you expected to see?	
	Did the written statements and the figures and ratios tell the same story?	
	What is your overall evaluation of the business?	

Having completed some competitor analysis, you will now have a good feeling for the levels of cost and profits you are likely to achieve in your business opportunity. We can use this information later when producing budgets and cash flow forecasts for your business plan, to check your figures are realistic.

THE CASH FLOW STATEMENT

The Cash Flow Statement is a tricky statement to understand. There are two allowed formats:

- The first is simply a list of cash transactions: sales income and expenditure. While this format is actually quite intuitive to understand, being very similar to your bank statement, it is not commonly used.

- The second is the most common format which we will examine here.

This format starts from the operating profit figure from the Profit and Loss Account and then makes adjustments to turn this from profit to cash. This may seem a complicated way of presenting the information, however most computer accounting systems are set up to account on an accruals basis (when costs are incurred as opposed to when the cash moves).

If you consider the operating profit line on the Profit and Loss Account, everything up until that point may bear no relation to real cash movements.

DIFFERENCES BETWEEN PROFIT AND CASH

- Sales are counted when the goods or services are delivered, not when the customer pays, so there would be a difference between profit and cash.

- Cost of sales are the costs of goods sold. More may have been bought and held in stock, and the cost of sales may not have been invoiced yet; they may have been bought on credit. So again there would be a difference between profit and cash.

- Overheads may include accruals (for costs incurred but not yet paid for) and provisions. Provisions are a recognition of a cost incurred, but not yet completely quantifiable – consider if an employee has an accident on your site and takes the company to court for compensation. The accident has happened, but at this stage, you can only estimate the compensation. You would have to account for the cost incurred, as an estimate. This would be called a provision. Accruals and provisions by definition have not been paid and therefore reflect a difference between profit and cash.

- Depreciation is listed in the overheads, but it is not a cash item. It's another difference between profit and cash.

- The operating profit line in the Profit and Loss Account is above interest and tax, so any interest or tax paid would not have been taken into account yet, so again, there is a difference between profit and cash.

- Dividends are not shown on the published Profit and Loss Account, but dividends are paid out of net profits. So again these are not reflected in the operating profit. Yet another difference between profit and cash.

- There are a number of items that don't make it onto the Profit and Loss Account at all, for example, fixed assets purchased, loans taken out or paid off, etc. These again have to be taken account of to get from profit to cash.

In this section we'll explain how the Cash Flow Statement is compiled, to help you to understand the layout of the Cash Flow Statements that you need to analyse.

Here are the steps required to move from operating profit to cash:

1. Start with operating profit from the Profit and Loss Account.

2. Add back depreciation. This was not a cash item. We're trying to move from profit to cash, so we will add back non-cash items.

3. If there is an increase in debtors from last year's Balance Sheet to this year's, the company must have collected less money from customers. These sales have been counted in the operating profit, so we must deduct this to get to a cash figure (and vice versa).

4. If there is an increase in creditors from last year's Balance Sheet to this year's, then the company must have paid fewer creditors than is accounted for in the cost of sales. The adjustment would be a positive to move from profit to cash (and vice versa).

5. If stock has increased from last year's Balance Sheet to this year's, then more stock has been bought, which represents a cash outflow and a negative adjustment to the operating profit (and vice versa).

6. Finally make negative adjustments to the operating profit for any interest, tax, dividends paid, fixed assets acquired, loans paid, etc. Make positive adjustments to operating profit for any loans taken out, shares sold, etc.

COACHING SESSION 19

Compile your own Cash Flow Statement

Let's try it out. From the Profit and Loss Account and Balance Sheet for ABC Company Ltd, try to compile the Cash Flow Statement below:

Cash Flow Statement for ABC Company Ltd for the year ended 31/12/2013

	£
Operating profit	
Add back depreciation and amortization	
Less increase in stock	
Add decrease in debtors	
Less decrease in creditors	
= Operating cash flow	
Less interest paid	
Less dividends paid	
Less tax paid	
Less loan paid off	
Less payments to acquire fixed assets	
Plus overdraft used	
= Net cash flow	

Check your answer here:

Cash Flow Statement for ABC Company Ltd for the year ended 31/12/2013

	£	Notes
Operating profit	200,000	Straight from the P&L
Add back depreciation and amortization	100,000	Straight from the P&L
Less increase in stock	(5,000)	Compare the two stock figures for 2012 and 2013 on the Balance Sheet in the current assets
Add decrease in debtors	7,000	Compare the two debtors figures for 2012 and 2013 on the Balance Sheet in the current assets
Less decrease in creditors	(5,000)	Compare the two creditors figures for 2012 and 2013 on the Balance Sheet in the current assets
= Operating cash flow	297,000	Total up the figures to this point
Less interest paid	(20,000)	The interest is listed on the P&L, but we should check that it was actually paid! If it had not been paid it would be listed in the Balance Sheet as a liability. In this case it was not listed as a liability, so it must have been paid.
Less dividends paid	(50,000)	The dividends proposed are listed on the P&L. However, we're trying to find out what cash was paid out in 2013. The dividends were proposed after the year end after the P&L was compiled, so could not have been paid in 2013. Check the Balance Sheet and you can see this year's proposed dividends are listed as a liability. So they must have paid last year's dividends during this year.
Less tax paid	(50,000)	The tax due is listed on the P&L. However, we're trying to find out what cash was paid out in 2013. The tax was calculated after the year end after the P&L was compiled, so could not have been paid in 2013. Check the Balance Sheet and you can see this year's tax is listed as a liability. So they must have paid last year's tax during this year.
Less loan paid off	(132,000)	Compare the loan figures for 2013 and 2012 on the Balance Sheet in the long-term liabilities.
Less payments to acquire fixed assets	(150,000)	If you thought the assets bought were £100k worth, you have not taken into account the depreciation. If the company had bought no assets, the £200k for 2012 would have depreciated by £50k to £150k in 2013. The actual figure for 2013 is £300k, therefore £150k of assets were bought.
Plus overdraft used	5,000	Compare the overdraft figures for 2013 and 2012 on the Balance Sheet in the current liabilities
= Net cash flow	(100,000)	Total up the column to this point

We can confirm that this is correct because the difference between cash on the Balance Sheet for 2012 and 2013 is £100k.

You may be wondering why we bothered with a Cash Flow Statement if it was clear how cash had moved from the Balance Sheet. The answer is that we can see much more from the Cash Flow Statement than by just looking at the Profit and Loss Account and Balance Sheet alone.

ANALYSING THE CASH FLOW STATEMENT

The way to analyse this Cash Flow Statement is to look firstly at whether all the profits were turned to cash. Not forgetting that depreciation is not a cash item, so we hope to see operating profit + depreciation = operating cash flow. In this case the operating profit plus depreciation is £300k and the operating cash flow is £297k. This is not far off, so we're not too worried. The company has paid more creditors (not very efficient) and taken on more stock (not very efficient either) but has collected more from its debtors which partly offsets this.

Moving to the next section of the Cash Flow Statement, we see that the company has paid interest and tax; there's not much to comment on there.

The company also paid dividends, which is strange as it has had to take out an overdraft. A smaller dividend would have negated the need for an overdraft. We must be concerned about their cash management!

However, most of the cash generated went into buying fixed assets, which is a productive thing and paying off a loan which is good for gearing. So all in all, most of the cash was used wisely in this year.

One thing to check is what type of assets were bought. If you look at the Balance Sheet, there will always be a note number against the fixed assets. Look up the note and you will likely see assets grouped into categories and you'll see the original costs, acquisitions, disposals and depreciation. If money was spent on buildings or machines, or any kind of productive asset, this is a good thing as it provides more capacity for more profits in the future.

If the assets bought were fixtures and fittings (i.e. a refurbishment or worse still, a fountain in reception) then there will be no return on this investment and the money is lost.

→ NEXT STEPS

In this chapter you have:

- Looked at how to understand and analyse the financial statements for your customers, suppliers and competitors

- Used this information to establish the size of the market, cost and profitability levels that are possible and to benchmark against your competitors' operations.

In the next chapter you will think about what return you and your investors can expect on your investment. You will look at your budgets and get started on some cash flow forecasts, to keep your investors happy.

TAKEAWAYS

This is your opportunity to take stock of what you have learned from this chapter. You might now want to choose other chapters and exercises to focus on, or you can continue to work through the whole book if this better fits your needs.

What did you learn about company accounts that surprised you?

What did you learn about your likely costs from looking at your competitors? Did anything surprise you?

Are you confident that your customers will be able to pay you? Which ratios gave you confidence in your customers? Did any of the ratios cause you concern?

Did you uncover any issues relating to your suppliers?

Which other competitors, customers or suppliers do you need to analyse to discover more about your industry?

THE FINANCIALS – EVALUATE YOUR BUSINESS OPPORTUNITY AND MANAGE YOUR BUSINESS

✔ OUTCOMES FROM THIS CHAPTER

- In this chapter we will evaluate your opportunity to establish what return you and your investors can expect on your investment. We will also produce budgets and cash flow forecasts to manage your finances and to share with investors.

EVALUATE THE OPPORTUNITY

Now it's time to make the final financial decision: is the opportunity worth it financially? First there are some things we need to consider in terms of what costs we need to include. For this we can use the acronym RICH:

- **Relevant:** Costs and incomes included in the financial evaluation must be relevant. Any costs that have already been spent are now 'sunk' costs and therefore irrelevant and not to be included. For example, imagine you have already spent £15,000 on some market research and now you're ready to make an informed decision. The £15,000 is spent and cannot be 'un-spent', so it is irrelevant to your decision now. You should disregard this cost in your calculations

- **Incremental:** Costs and incomes included in the financial evaluation must be incurred as a direct result of the decision. If you are looking to run this new project from your current office, there is no need to include allocated overheads (such as rent of the building, utilities, etc.) in the calculation. These costs will be incurred whether you decide to proceed with the opportunity or not. However, if there is no room for the new project team in the existing office and you will use a porta-cabin hired in specially, then the costs of this must be included.

- **Cash:** Costs and incomes must be counted when the cash actually flows, rather than on the profit (or accruals) basis. The profits from your opportunity may look really good, but if all the cash inflows happen at the end of the project, there is a time cost of money and in real cash terms this may affect your decision.

- **Holistic:** Costs and incomes arising from the project must be included. Say for example that you are getting some 'free' resource, such as a secondee from another department. While this is free resource for your project, if the secondee is being replaced by a temporary employee in their normal job, this is a cost of running the project. Take costs incurred anywhere in the business into account for this evaluation.

COACHING SESSION 20

Cash flow forecast

The first thing we need to do is to put together a cash flow forecast for the opportunity. Take account of all cash flows into and out of the business when the cash actually moves. Take into account any up-front investment used to get the project started in Time 0, then count all other costs and incomes in the relevant years that the cash flows (in Times 1–10) in the following template:

Financial evaluation of business opportunity

Description	Time										
	0	1	2	3	4	5	6	7	8	9	10
Cash Inflows											
Total additional cash inflow A											
Cash Outflows											
Total additional cash outflow B											
Net cash flow (A–B)											

There are five different methods of financially evaluating projects. We'll look at all of them here because different businesses and investors will be interested in different tools. In order to review them all, including the benefits and drawbacks of each, we will compare two different example projects. The two projects both involve an up-front investment of £50k. Project A only lasts for two years and thereafter there are no further cash flows. Project B lasts for five years.

For the purposes of illustration here, we have summarized the cash flows into a single stream, the total of all cash inflows and cash outflows for each time period (i.e. the total figures at the bottom of the chart above).

Time	Project A	Project B
0	−50,000	−50,000
1	35,000	20,000
2	35,000	20,000
3		20,000
4		30,000
5		40,000

BENEFIT:COST ANALYSIS

The first method we will examine is the benefit:cost ratio. In order to calculate this ratio, we simply add up all the up-front costs and compare them to the net cash inflows over the life of the project:

	Project A	Project B
Benefit:cost ratio	70:50	130:50
If you then divide both sides by the up-front investment, you can see the ratio as ?:1	1.4:1	2.6:1
Or we can express this as a percentage of benefits over costs	40%	160%

There is no formal agreement on how the benefit:cost ratio is displayed, so any of the three formats is acceptable

If the benefit exceeds the cost, then the project is accepted.

Benefits

The method is very simple to calculate and to communicate.

Drawbacks

Because this method takes no account of when the cash flows, it may lead you to accept a project where all the cash inflows are at the end, by which time your business may have gone into liquidation! For longer term-investments, this is not a good tool.

Why would you use this method?

For short-term projects, this method is fine and no further analysis is needed. If the benefits exceed the costs within two to three years, then it can be considered a 'no-brainer'.

PAYBACK PERIOD

The next method we will look at is the payback period. This is a time-based method that simply looks at how long in time it takes for the cash inflows to equal the cash outflows (i.e. for the project to break even). For our example above the payback periods are:

	Project A	Project B
Method	The initial investment is £50k. During year 1 there is a net cash inflow of £35k. This is not enough to pay back the initial investment, but the cash inflow of £35k in year 2 does finally pay back the initial investment.	The initial investment is £50k. During year 1 there is a net cash inflow of £20k, after two and a half years the cash inflows equal the investment.
Payback period	In year 2	In year 3

If the payback period is less than the company's target, then the project is accepted.

Benefits

This method is really simple to calculate and to communicate.

The method drives us to be concerned with cash flow, so we accept projects that pay back more quickly. Then we'll have cash coming in early that we can re-invest into other projects.

To some extent, the method takes account of risk. When forecasting the cash flows of a project, which figures are more accurate; the first years, or the later years? Of course the earlier years are likely to be more certain: the longer a project goes on the more risks may occur, so the cash flow forecasts of later years are less certain. The payback method drives us to choose projects that pay back quickly and so we eliminate later, riskier cash flows from our decision.

Drawbacks

This method is short-sighted, in that we ignore cash flows after the payback period. The two projects above are difficult to choose between intuitively. However, if project B actually lasted for ten years and the cash flows grew every year from year six to year ten, intuitively, we might think project B is the better. But the payback period method would ignore this and still drive us to choose project A.

Why would you use this method?

This is a quick and simple method to calculate and will give you a good rule of thumb; if the project pays back in a few short years, then it will be of interest and we may use some more sophisticated methods to analyse further.

The types of company that tend to rely more heavily this method are those that are either a) risk averse (and so like to generate cash flows quickly before any risks occur) or b) have limited access to capital and so require projects to pay back quickly in order to fund future projects.

RETURN ON INVESTMENT/ACCOUNTING RATE OF RETURN

The next method we will look at is the Return on Investment – although, there is no such actual term! If someone asks to see a Return on Investment calculation, they may want to see any or all of the methods shown in this section, or maybe they are looking for the Accounting Rate of Return method. This is the method we'll use now:

	Project A	Project B
Method: $$\frac{\text{average annual profit}}{\text{initial investment}} \times 100$$		
Accounting Rate of Return	$\frac{35,000}{50,0000} \times 100 = 70\%$	$\frac{26,000}{50,0000} \times 100 = 52\%$

If the Accounting Rate of Return is higher than the company's target, then the project is accepted.

Benefits

This method is really simple to calculate and to communicate and most people conceptually like the idea of a % return; it fits with a comparison of the total company's Return on Capital Employed (ROCE) or even a comparison with the interest rate that you could achieve by leaving the money invested instead.

Drawbacks

This is not a good method for decision making, for the following reasons:

- Firstly, it uses average annual profits (when our rule was to use cash. In this example we used cash for simplicity rather than calculating the profit by depreciating the up-front investment over the life of the project).

- Secondly, it averages out the profits further. In our discussion on payback we said that later cash flows may be more risky, but this method has smoothed the lumpy cash flows into an average annual figure, thereby negating some of the risk that we project cash flows will start small and grow in later years!

Why would you use this method?

If the project's ARR is greater than the company's existing ROCE, then it would appear that the project will improve the company's results over the life of the project.

Take the results with a pinch of salt though! Take a look at the following example:

Time	Project C	Project D
0	–10,000	–10,000
1	4,000	4,000
2	4,000	4,000
3		4,000
4		4,000
5		4,000
ARR	40%	40%

While both projects seem to give an accounting rate of return of 40%, the first project doesn't even pay back! This method can be quite misleading.

NET PRESENT VALUE (NPV)

Net Present Value is by far the best method for evaluating longer-term projects, business plans and anything that requires a larger investment in the early stages. The reason is that it uses cash flows (unlike ARR), it takes account of the complete project life (unlike the payback period) and it takes account of the time value of money (unlike the benefit:cost ratio).

What do we mean by 'time value of money'? Would you rather be given £100 today, or £100 in a year's time? Clearly you'd want the money now. If you wanted to spend the money, what you could buy today with £100 is probably more than you could buy in one year from today because of *inflation*. In addition, if you wanted to invest your £100, it would be worth more than £100 in one year from today because of *interest*. The effect of interest and inflation means that money is worth more today than in the future.

Say we could invest our £100 today at a 10% interest rate; in one year from today it would be worth £110. In our example, we don't have cash today. We have cash flowing in over the next few years. If we had £110 arriving one year from today, what would it be worth in today's money? This is the process we're going to use now. Looking at project A, one year from today we have £35k flowing in. What is that worth in today's values? Assuming a cost of capital (the cost to us of interest or dividends of using money invested in our business) of 10%, we'll discount the future cash flows from each project to state them in today's values. This is the method we'll use now:

Time	Discount factor @ 10%	Project A	Discounted cash flow	Project B	Discounted cash flow
0	1	−50,000	−50,000	−50,000	−50,000
1	0.909	35,000	31,815	20,000	18,180
2	0.826	35,000	28,910	20,000	16,520
3	0.751			20,000	15,020
4	0.683			30,000	20,490
5	0.621			40,000	24,840
NPV			10,725		45,050

We'll come back to the discount factor and explain how that is calculated shortly, but for now, just understand that money today (at time 0) is worth its face value, so the discount factor we use is 1. Simply multiply the £50k project A investment by the discount factor of 1. £50k today is worth £50k today.

But £35k flowing into the business in year 1 is worth a little less to us. Using a 10% discount rate, the discount factor for year 1 is 0.909. This simply means that £1 in a year's time is the equivalent of almost 91p today. If we invested 91p today at 10%, in a year's time we'd have £1.

Multiply the £35k flowing into the business in year 1 by 0.909 and we see that the discounted cash flow (i.e. the cash flow in today's values) is £31,815.

We continue to multiply all the actual cash flows by the discount factor to determine the discounted cash flow (the value of the actual cash flow in today's money terms).

The final step is to total up the discounted cash flow column.

Project A has an NPV of £10,725. This means that if we accept project A, we will have £10,725 more than if we do not implement project A. It is a positive value, so the project is worthwhile. However, Project B has a greater NPV, so it is the better project. The cash flows have been discounted, so even though the two projects have different lives, we can compare the them completely fairly.

> **! COACH'S TIP**
>
> ### Exploring NPV further
>
> If you'd like more information on this subject, there is an excellent description of the method in *Finance for Managers* (see Bibliography). If you'd like a more in-depth review of how to value different business options, then *Real Options* by Amram and Kulatilaka (see Bibliography) is a good source.

If the NPV is greater than 0, then the project is accepted. When comparing projects, the greater the NPV the better.

Benefits

This method is the most reliable method as it:

- uses cash flows (unlike ARR);
- takes account of the complete project life (unlike the payback period);
- takes account of the time value of money (unlike the benefit:cost ratio).

Drawbacks

There are no real drawbacks. We do need to know (or estimate) the cost of capital. While interest rates may fluctuate over time, we cannot wait for perfect information (or it will be too late, we'll have missed our opportunity) so it's not too important to estimate the cost of capital very accurately, simply build in a little space for risk in the discount factor used, i.e. add a little to the real cost of capital to compensate for risk.

Why would you use this method?

The NPV tells you exactly how much cash *in today's values* you will have at the end of the time frame evaluated. As such this is a really good evaluation method.

THE DISCOUNT FACTOR

For the purposes of your business plan, you really only need to understand NPV conceptually, as you can download a spreadsheet at www.TYCoachbooks.com/Businessplans that will calculate all the evaluation results for you.

However, we said we'd come back to the discount factor and also how to determine your cost of capital (i.e. what discount factor should we use?) So if you feel you need to understand this, we'll review it now:

The discount factor is calculated by the formula $1/1+r$, where r is the discount factor, so in our example where we used 10%, the formula is $1/1.1 = 0.909$. If we take $0.909/1.1 = 0.826$ and so on for each year. Or if you prefer $1/(1+r)^n$ where 'n' is the number of the year you wish to calculate.

Below there is a table provided for you that lists all the discount factors for up to ten years at every cost of capital.

But, more importantly, how do we determine the 'cost of capital' that we wish to use? The cost of capital should strictly be the true cost of capital. The capital employed in your business is all the money invested by owners (total equity), plus long-term loans (both of which you can pick up straight from the Balance Sheet) compared to the cost of this capital (all the interest paid on loans plus all the dividends paid). The cost of capital as a percentage of capital employed is your true cost of capital. However, most businesses will increase this for decision-making purposes. For example if a company's true cost of capital is 6%, they may increase it to as much as 12%, partly to provide a buffer in case interest rates fluctuate, and partly to encourage investment in projects that provide much more profit than just covering the cost of capital and finally to take account of risk. Higher discount factors will reduce much faster over time, so will discount the later, riskier cash flows more than lower discount factors, the result being a lower NPV for the project.

If you're currently in business, putting together a business plan to gain approval for a project from your senior managers, then your finance department will be able to tell you exactly what discount factor to use. Alternative terms that your company may use for discount factor are: 'cost of capital' or 'hurdle rate'.

If you're an entrepreneur, putting together a business plan to start a completely new business, then either use the discount factor your funders favour, or take a middle of the road rate of around 12%. If the business is risky, you could also evaluate at 15% to test the sensitivity. If your business idea provides a positive NPV at 15%, it is quite impervious to risk. This might be quite persuasive for investors!

DISCOUNT TABLE

Here is a table showing all the discount factors for up to ten years for each level of cost of capital:

Discount table

Cost of capital	time 0	time 1	time 2	time 3	time 4	time 5	time 6	time 7	time 8	time 9	time 10
1%	1	0.9901	0.9803	0.9706	0.9610	0.9515	0.9420	0.9327	0.9235	0.9143	0.9053
2%	1	0.9804	0.9612	0.9423	0.9238	0.9057	0.8880	0.8706	0.8535	0.8368	0.8203
3%	1	0.9709	0.9426	0.9151	0.8885	0.8626	0.8375	0.8131	0.7894	0.7664	0.7441
4%	1	0.9615	0.9246	0.8890	0.8548	0.8219	0.7903	0.7599	0.7307	0.7026	0.6756
5%	1	0.9524	0.9070	0.8638	0.8227	0.7835	0.7462	0.7107	0.6768	0.6446	0.6139
6%	1	0.9434	0.8900	0.8396	0.7921	0.7473	0.7050	0.6651	0.6274	0.5919	0.5584
7%	1	0.9346	0.8734	0.8163	0.7629	0.7130	0.6663	0.6227	0.5820	0.5439	0.5083
8%	1	0.9259	0.8573	0.7938	0.7350	0.6806	0.6302	0.5835	0.5403	0.5002	0.4632
9%	1	0.9174	0.8417	0.7722	0.7084	0.6499	0.5963	0.5470	0.5019	0.4604	0.4224
10%	1	0.9091	0.8264	0.7513	0.6830	0.6209	0.5645	0.5132	0.4665	0.4241	0.3855
11%	1	0.9009	0.8116	0.7312	0.6587	0.5935	0.5346	0.4817	0.4339	0.3909	0.3522
12%	1	0.8929	0.7972	0.7118	0.6355	0.5674	0.5066	0.4523	0.4039	0.3606	0.3220
13%	1	0.8850	0.7831	0.6931	0.6133	0.5428	0.4803	0.4251	0.3762	0.3329	0.2946
14%	1	0.8772	0.7695	0.6750	0.5921	0.5194	0.4556	0.3996	0.3506	0.3075	0.2697
15%	1	0.8696	0.7561	0.6575	0.5718	0.4972	0.4323	0.3759	0.3269	0.2843	0.2472
16%	1	0.8621	0.7432	0.6407	0.5523	0.4761	0.4104	0.3538	0.3050	0.2630	0.2267
17%	1	0.8547	0.7305	0.6244	0.5337	0.4561	0.3898	0.3332	0.2848	0.2434	0.2080
18%	1	0.8475	0.7182	0.6086	0.5158	0.4371	0.3704	0.3139	0.2660	0.2255	0.1911
19%	1	0.8403	0.7062	0.5934	0.4987	0.4190	0.3521	0.2959	0.2487	0.2090	0.1756
20%	1	0.8333	0.6944	0.5787	0.4823	0.4019	0.3349	0.2791	0.2326	0.1938	0.1615

INTERNAL RATE OF RETURN (IRR)

Internal rate of return is a very similar method to NPV. It is based on the same concept, but it is a % return measure.

With NPV we took the forecasted cash flows for a project, and applied a discount factor to calculate an NPV for the project. What if we didn't know the discount factor to use? We could pick a discount factor that would force the NPV to zero. If you like, it's the break-even cost of capital. If interest rates rise and rise, how far do they have to go before the project's NPV = 0, i.e. the project neither makes nor loses money. That interest rate would be the IRR.

In order to estimate this value, we can calculate the NPV at a discount factor of 10% as before, then (as both projects were positive at 10%) we could increase the discount factor by a large amount to see if we can force it to a negative NPV; let's try 30%:

Time	Discount factor @ 10%	Discount factor (@30%)	Project A	Discounted cash flow (@ 10%)	Discounted cash flow (@30%)	Project B	Discounted cash flow (@10%)	Discounted cash flow (@30%)
0	1	1	−50,000	−50,000	−50,000	−50,000	−50,000	−50,000
1	0.909	0.769	35,000	31,815	26,915	20,000	18,180	15,380
2	0.826	0.592	35,000	28,910	20,720	20,000	16,520	11,840
3	0.751	0.455				20,000	15,020	9,100
4	0.683	0.350				30,000	20,490	10,500
5	0.621	0.269				40,000	24,840	10,760
NPV				10,725	-2,365		45,050	7,580

The final step is to estimate, using the two values calculated, the point at which the NPV is zero. For Project A, plot on the graph the NPV at 10% (i.e. 10,725) and the NPV at 30% (i.e. −2,365) and draw a line between the two. The NPV is zero where the line crosses the x axis at the discount factor of 26%, i.e. at a discount factor of 26% the NPV is zero, the Internal Rate of Return is 26%.

Do the same for Project B and we see that at both discount factors the NPVs are positive. Simply plot both values, then extrapolate the line until it crosses the x axis (at 36%), i.e. the IRR of project B is 36%. The cost of capital would have to rise to 36% before the project becomes unviable. This is the better project, as it has the higher IRR. As the IRR is so high, at 36%, we can judge that the project will still be viable if risks occur, so it is a very robust project.

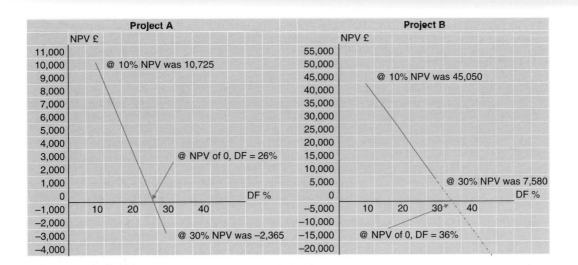

Benefits

This method is still very reliable as it is based on the same concept as NPV.

Some companies and investors prefer this method, as they prefer a percentage return.

Drawbacks

There is a flaw in IRR in that it can only calculate an IRR for a single change in direction of cash flow. There is a separate IRR for every change in direction of cash flow, so looking at the project below where, for example, a house is bought, then rented out, then requires refurbishment in year 4, then returns to positive cash flows, we cannot calculate an IRR for the whole project:

Time	Cash flows
0	−100k
1	25k
2	25k
3	25k
4	-50k
5	25k
6	25k
7	25k
8	25k
9	25k
10	25k

In this case, it is better to rely on the NPV and ignore the IRR.

Why would you use this method?

Many investors like to see a percentage return and therefore prefer an IRR. If you calculate all the measures we've looked at in this section, then your investors or senior managers can make a balanced decision from all the tools available.

PRODUCE A CASH FLOW FORECAST AND BUDGET

Cash flow forecast

Actually, you've already completed your cash flow forecast as part of the evaluation. If you downloaded and completed the tool, then the spreadsheet you completed for the evaluation has a third tab, which has formatted your cash flow forecast for you. You simply need to print it out to show your investors.

There is another tab called monthly cash flow forecast, if you want to break your first year's cash flow into a monthly projection for more information. If you're going to the banks or other investors for funding, they may well ask to see a monthly cash flow forecast.

A key point to focus on here, as part of our cash flow forecasting is working capital management. We mentioned working capital in the previous chapter, when looking at the Balance Sheet; however, how we manage this is critical to the business. Working capital is such an important subject; poor management of working capital is one of the main reasons for business failure. Let's look at it in a different way through an example:

Imagine you have a manufacturing business where on average:

- Raw materials are held in stock for four weeks prior to production.
- Production takes two weeks.
- Finished goods are held for six weeks.
- Debtors take 60 days (eight weeks) to pay.

Here's the same example shown in a timeline:

Weeks																			
1	2	3	4	5	6	7	8	9	10	11	12	13	14	15	16	17	18	19	20

Raw Mats — Prod'n — Finished Goods — Debtors

Goods received — Prod'n complete — Customer pays

Production starts

Invoice raised, goods delivered

In this example, if we paid for everything up front, then cash paid out would be tied up in the working capital cycle for 20 weeks (or five months) before the money was received from the customer.

However it's very unlikely that we would pay for everything up front. Credit terms are usually agreed with suppliers:

- Raw materials creditors have given us credit terms of 60 days (eight weeks).
- Production staff are paid monthly.
- Overheads are paid monthly.

Let's add this information to our timeline:

Weeks																			
1	2	3	4	5	6	7	8	9	10	11	12	13	14	15	16	17	18	19	20

Raw Mats — Prod'n — Finished Goods — Debtors

Raw Mats Creditors — Cash tied up in raw mats - 3 mths

Prod'n Staff — Cash tied up in labour - 3 mths

Overheads — Cash tied up in overheads - 4 months

The key time frames to note here are the periods of time the cash is tied up in the working capital cycle until the money is received from the customer.

A key point to note is that many people think that as long as your creditor days (the time taken to pay suppliers) is longer than your debtor days (the time taken to collect cash from the customer) then your cash will be positive. This is clearly not true, because it ignores the length of time that the stock is held! Here in our example the debtor and creditor days are the same, but cash is tied up in raw materials for three months because of the time taken in stock holding and production.

We can further calculate how much money we would need to fund our working capital cycle.

While this single illustrated timeline only looks at a single iteration through the working capital cycle, we know that we don't run one working capital cycle from start to finish and then start the next one. Instead we receive materials in every day, we start production every day, we finish goods and send them to the warehouse every day, we make deliveries every day and we receive payment in from customers every day. Likewise we're making payments to creditors every day.

Think about it, if we overlay our timeline with many more timelines starting each day, at any point in time, on any day of the year, we'd have about three months' worth of money tied up in raw materials, about three months' worth of money tied up in labour costs and about four months' worth of money tied up in overheads.

If you know your budget for a year, we can calculate how much money is required to fund the working capital cycle. Let's say that our annual budget is:

Raw materials	£1,000k
Labour	£ 800k
Overheads	£ 600k

If we plan to spend £1,000k on raw materials in a year and we know that at any time we have about three months' worth of money tied up in raw materials, then we need only multiply £1,000k by 3 months out of 12, i.e.
£1,000k × 3 / 12 = £250k

If we plan to spend £800k on labour in a year and we know that at any time we have about three months' worth of money tied up in labour costs, then
£800k × 3 / 12 = £200k

Finally, if we plan to spend £600k on overheads and at any time we have four months' worth of money tied up in overheads, then £600k × 4 / 12 = £200k

In total we need £650k cash to keep the working capital cycle running.

Finally, anything that can be done to improve the working capital cycle will reduce the investment required.

For example, if raw materials are delivered in closer to just in time, if production is made faster and more efficient, if goods are delivered out to customers more quickly and so held in stock for less time, if customers can be persuaded to pay more quickly and if we can negotiate longer payment terms with suppliers:

Weeks																			
1	2	3	4	5	6	7	8	9	10	11	12	13	14	15	16	17	18	19	20
Raw Mats				Prod'n			Finished Goods						Debtors						
Raw Mats Creditors																			

If we were able to reduce the working capital cycle as suggested in the timeline above, from raw material delivery to payment from the customer is ten weeks, yet our terms with our suppliers are now twelve weeks. We'd be receiving the money from the customer before we had to pay our raw materials supplier! We'd be funding our business using creditors' money, just like the Amazon example in Chapter 7 which would hugely improve cash management and give more breathing space if customers are slow to pay.

! COACH'S TIP

Read the small print

Ensure that you are completely aware of the contracted payment terms and lead times in your business and when forecasting your cash flow remember to take these into account.

Budget

When budgeting, it's a good idea to follow a process to organize your thoughts:

Step	Notes	Example
1. Objectives	Remember your objectives from Chapter 1? We need to review these in order to determine how they will affect the budget. What do you actually want to achieve, in what timeframe? Start with your five-year objectives, then break these down into some annual objectives.	Let's say you're a professional institute and your objective is to double membership in five years. You currently have 120,000 members and the training process for new members takes three years. You currently train around 3,000 students a year.
2. Limiting factor	Step two is to identify what will stop you achieving your objectives (these are your limiting factors). It's important to understand what the bottlenecks are in your objectives; these will need to be overcome in order to achieve your objectives and planning for this will help you to put your budget together. There may be more than one limiting factor, you will need to run through each and plan for each.	What will stop you from doubling membership? Student numbers will probably be the main limiting factor. How many graduates will want to train in your profession? Your options are to: ● Increase recruitment efforts ● Recruit students from other institutes ● Give reciprocal membership to overseas institutes ● Acquire or merge with another institute
3. First part of your budget	The next step is to put together a budget for the critical plans you've put in place for overcoming your limiting factors.	Will any one of the options fulfil your objectives, or will you need to implement a mix of options or all options? Put plans in place to work out how you will go about this and budget accordingly. What are your operational plans? What resources will you need? What will this cost and what income will this bring in?
4. The rest of your budget	The rest of your budget should just fall out of your existing plans.	Once you know how many students you'll attract, you will know how many registrations, how many sets of learning materials, how many exam places, etc. that you will need. Budget for all steps of your operational process.

Step	Notes	Example
5. Present and negotiate your budget	If you have to go back to your investors or your senior managers to present your budget, then present it in the same way: ● Slide one reminds them of the overall objectives for your five-year plan and the objectives for this year ● Slide two describes how you will achieve your objectives: what you will do, what resources you need, and what the incomes and costs will be. ● Only then get into the detail of the budget numbers.	If your investors or managers challenge your budget, you can now review the objectives and your plans. Discuss and agree if any of your plans can be delayed, or changed, without affecting the objectives
6. Agree the budget	Finalize your agreed budget.	
7. Monitor and review	Each month, check progress on your operational plans – are you achieving against your timelines, and review your budget – are you on track? If not, what can you do to get back to budget?	

Returning to our spreadsheet, already completed for the project evaluation and cash flow, the fourth tab gives you a format to put together a budget. Remember, your budget will take account of incomes and costs when they are incurred, as opposed to when the cash actually flows.

Tabs five to ten set your budget out by month for the first half of the year with space for you to enter your actual incomes and costs to keep track of your achievements compared to budget. Simply copy the templates into new tabs for a full year.

The format is shown below:

Budget Report for the month of:	February				Year to Date			
Income	Budget	Actual	Variance	Vari %	Budget	Actual	Variance	Vari %
Sales of product 1	20	15	−5	−25%	40	30	−10	−25%
Sales of product 2	20	10	−10	−50%	40	20	−20	−50%
Sales of product 3	20	30	10	50%	40	40	0	0%
	0	0	0	0%	0	0	0	0%
	0	0	0	0%	0	0	0	0%
Total Income	60	55	−5	−8%	120	90	−30	−25%
Expenditure								
Raw Materials	5	10	−5	−100%	10	20	−10	−100%
Assembly Labour	5	10	−5	−100%	10	20	−10	−100%
Distribution	6	3	3	50%	12	6	6	50%
Rent & rates	4	1	3	75%	8	1	7	88%
Admin	5	7	−2	−40%	10	8	2	20%
Consumables	3	2	1	33%	6	5	1	17%
Other	0	0	0	0%	0	0	0	0%
Total Expenditure	28	33	−5	−18%	56	60	−4	−7%
Net Profit	32	22	−10	−31%	64	30	−34	−53%

ONLINE RESOURCE

Budget

A downloadable budget template is available at:

www.TYCoachbooks.com/Businessplans

NEXT STEPS

In this chapter you have:

- Evaluated your opportunity to understand for yourself the costs and benefits of the opportunity and to communicate to investors what returns they can expect.

- Prepared cash flow forecasts and budgets to help you to manage the opportunity and to give confidence to investors that you are in control.

- Focused on working capital and ensured that you have taken credit terms with customers and suppliers as well as delivery lead times into account in your cash flow forecast.

In the next chapter you will think about how you are going to fund your venture. Do you need short-term or long-term funding? The type of funding you secure may affect how much control you have over your business, so it's important you consider very carefully how much control of your business you are prepared to hand over.

TAKEAWAYS

This is your opportunity to take stock of what you have learned from this chapter. You might now want to choose other chapters and exercises to focus on, or you can continue to work through the whole book if this better fits your needs.

Do you now have an understanding of what returns you can expect for your opportunity?

Do your expected returns fulfil your investors'/senior managers' expectations?

Now you've completed your financial evaluation, do you need to amend your plans to improve your returns?

Now you've completed your budget do you need to amend your plans to manage your performance better?

Now you've completed your cash flow forecast, do you need to reconsider payment terms or processes to improve your cash flow?

Is there anything that surprised you in this chapter?

How often do you plan to review your actual performance against budget in order to maintain control? Who do you need to share this information with?

9 GAINING FUNDING

- In this chapter, we'll look at different sources of funding, the difference between short-term and long-term funding, the benefits and drawbacks for each type of funding and how each type may affect your control of the business.

SHORT-TERM VS. LONG-TERM FUNDING

First, let's look at the difference between short-term funding and long-term funding.

The ideal is to match the length of the funding to the need. For short-term needs, such as covering a temporary cash flow issue or increasing working capital requirements, a short-term loan or overdraft is more appropriate. If you took out a long-term loan, while the interest rate in percentage terms may be lower, you'd actually pay more in interest over the life of the loan, and the need for the loan may have resolved itself in the early months of the loan term.

! COACH'S TIP

Plan ahead

Plan your finances (cash flow forecast and budget) carefully to establish not only how much funding you will need, but when you will need it too.

For longer-term needs, for example starting your business, growing your business, buying new machinery, etc., a long-term funding method is more appropriate.

In the case of a business start-up, it will take time for the business to grow to profitability, funding with delayed interest payments will suit a start-up as the payments will start to fall due as profitability is reached.

In the case of buying new equipment or machinery, it may take time for a new machine to be used to full capacity and that machine will generate profits over a long time period. So longer-term funding, with interest payments spread over the life of the machine, are more appropriate than a shorter-term loan. Even if you believe you could pay a shorter-term loan, it gives no room for manoeuvre if other issues arise.

! COACH'S TIP

The right fit

Fit the funding term to the need: long-term funding for start-up and asset purchase; short-term funding for cash flow and working capital needs.

COACHING SESSION 21

Reviewing the funding options

Let's review all the funding options now. The table below describes each option, the benefits and drawbacks and the impact on control:

Funding option	Description	Benefits	Drawbacks	Impact on control
Grants* (see Online resource box below for grant funding options)	This is an attractive option as many government agencies and charities may be able to fund a wide range of business activities, from start-up, funded apprenticeship schemes, Research and Development, training, etc.	It's free funding or subsidy for activities that you would have had to pay for anyway.	There may be complicated application and review processes. It may take time to gain the funding. The conditions of grants often include you having to match the funding from the grant, so you can only receive half of the full funds you need. There may be 'claw back' clauses if you don't fulfil your conditions.	In some cases, there may be conditions placed on the grant, affecting your plans, such as specification of outcomes.
Overdraft	An overdraft is a short-term facility agreed with your bank to temporarily spend more than the funds available in your account. A limit to the overdraft is agreed with the bank.	You only pay interest on the amount you use, as you use it. So it's much more flexible and cheaper than if you take out a loan to cover all your needs for a longer period of time. It's quick and easy to agree with the bank. There are no fees for paying it off (unlike with a fixed-term loan if you choose to pay it off early)	The interest rates and charges for using your overdraft facility can be higher than the interest charged on a fixed-term loan. You will be charged more if you go over your overdraft limit, you will probably have a one-off fee as you go over plus your interest will increase too. The bank can recall the overdraft at any time for any (or no) reason. There will usually be a charge if you want to extend your overdraft.	There is no loss of control or decision making.

Funding option	Description	Benefits	Drawbacks	Impact on control
Bank loans	Bank loans, or loans from public sources, can be for almost any time frame with any level of interest. It's important to establish your funding needs early to give you time to shop around and negotiate the best rates for you. Interest rates may be fixed, so it won't change over the life of the loan, giving you confidence and security. Interest rates may be variable, so it will change as the Bank of England changes its base rate, or as the lender's costs change.	The good thing about a loan is that it will have a fixed term and the bank cannot demand repayment early (unlike an overdraft). The lender has no control over your business activities and decision making nor will they take a share of your profits (unlike with shareholders).	There may be conditions on a loan, known as loan covenants, where the lender sets certain conditions, for example a cap on gearing, or target profitability levels. If these loan covenants are breached, the lender could demand repayment early. There may be charges if you want to repay the loan early. Loans may need to be secured against an asset, and if you struggle to make the interest payments, the lender may not be sympathetic and take the asset. If the value of the asset doesn't cover the outstanding loan value the lender may still pursue you for additional payments. If the interest rate charged is variable, you may struggle to plan and manage your finances.	There is little impact on control of your business and decision making unless you breach your loan covenants; read the terms of any loan carefully and seek legal advice before committing to any contracts, to ensure you understand any consequences in case of early repayment, breach of loan covenants or failure to make the interest payments.

Funding option	Description	Benefits	Drawbacks	Impact on control
Leasing (operating leases)	Here, instead of taking out a loan to buy an asset, you could instead lease the asset.	The leasing company has to maintain and repair the asset if it breaks down. Lease costs are fixed each month, giving you confidence in financial planning. At the end of the lease period you can give the asset back, buy it for a small fee, or replace the asset with a new lease. This is better for cash flow, spreading the costs, than buying outright with cash. Lease companies will often offer to continue to lease the asset to you after the initial term. It's important to negotiate a discount for extending the lease, as the lease company have covered their purchase costs by this point.	If you don't keep up payments you will lose the asset. You can only take out an operating lease on an asset, for example when buying a new machine, so it won't cover working capital requirements. You might not be able to get out of the contract early if your needs change. It is usually more expensive than owning the asset over the whole life of that asset.	No loss of control or decision making.

Funding option	Description	Benefits	Drawbacks	Impact on control
Selling shares in your business	Here, the investor takes ownership of a share of the company, shares part of the profits and may want to influence the business plan and business decisions.	Bringing in an investor with specific business skills may help you with ideas, contacts and business skills that you don't possess. There are no interest payments to be made. Dividend payments are voted on by all the shareholders, so depending on what share of the business you have sold, if you retain the controlling share, you will have ultimate control over whether a dividend is paid or not.	Finding investors and contracting with them can be difficult, time consuming and expensive. You lose: • some control of the business and decision making • some of the final sale value if the business is sold later • some of the profits. This is only an option if you are a limited company (private limited LTD, or public limited PLC) as sole traders and partnerships can't sell shares. See Chapter 5 for more information on different legal forms of companies).	Some control and decision making is lost depending on the size of the share of the business sold.

Funding option	Description	Benefits	Drawbacks	Impact on control
Private equity	Private equity finance is provided for a stake in the business. Usually only companies with potential for high growth are attractive to private equity investors. They are normally established businesses requiring some additional funding for growth, or needing specific expertise or to improve efficiency. The private equity firm raises funds from insurance companies and pension funds, individuals, etc. The private equity firm normally takes part in the management of the business funded. Private equity firms will normally have an exit strategy, to grow the business for a short period of a few years, then sell out for a profit.	You don't just gain funding, but also business acumen and any particular expertise needed to grow the business or to improve efficiency.	As with selling shares, you lose a great deal of control and decision making.	As above, a loss in control and decision making, depending on the size of the stake sold.

Funding option	Description	Benefits	Drawbacks	Impact on control
Venture capital	Venture capital firms are very similar to private equity firms, the only real difference is that they normally specialize in investing in new start-ups where there is no track record and cash needs are great.	As abcve	As above	As above
Factoring	With factoring, you sell your debtors (invoices owed to you by customers) to a factoring company who pay you a portion of the value, then they collect the money from the customer directly for themselves.	You receive cash up front as soon as you invoice instead of having to wait for customers to pay.	Depending on the factoring company you use, you could receive only 75–85% of the money. Customers may lose confidence and source alternative suppliers if they think you have cash flow problems, unless you tell them up front that this is your policy for all customers.	No loss of control or decision making. However, if customers don't pay, you have no involvement or understanding of the process the factoring company may use to collect. If their processes or their mistakes upset your customers, you may lose them.

ONLINE RESOURCE

Grant options

To review what grant options are available, look at:

https://www.gov.uk/business-finance-support-finder/search

COACH'S TIP

Don't leave it too late!

Don't forget to consider how your funding requirements may change if your opportunity takes off faster than you anticipated. Searching for funding late in the day when you are desperate for it, could leave you with few options, high interest rates or, worse still, no funding at all.

NEXT STEPS

In this chapter you have:

• Considered the advantages and disadvantages of different funding methods, particularly in terms of the impact on control of your business and the impact if you fail to make the payments.

In the next chapter you will look at which stakeholders in your business are going to have influence over your business plan. You'll take a close look at who these stakeholders are, and how you can best communicate with them to ensure their needs are met.

TAKEAWAYS

This is your opportunity to take stock of what you have learned from this chapter. You might now want to choose other chapters and exercises to focus on, or you can continue to work through the whole book if this better fits your needs.

Were you able to bring forward your financial planning from previous chapters to understand what your funding needs are?

Have you separated out all your long-term and short-term funding requirements?

What mix of funding methods have you chosen to ensure you retain your required level of control?

Have you found a mix of funding that allows you some flexibility in case of unforeseen events?

Did you identify in the review session how you will go about securing any funding you need?

PRESENTING YOUR PLAN

✔ OUTCOMES FROM THIS CHAPTER

- In this chapter we will identify all the stakeholders who will have some influence over your business plan. We will also look at each stakeholder group in turn and identify their objectives, attitudes and also their preferred communication style to ensure the plan covers all possible interests and objectives and that the presentation of the plan suits all communication styles.

STAKEHOLDER MAPPING

First, you'll need to identify all the people who could have an impact on your business plan. A useful tool for categorizing the individual stakeholders and stakeholder groups is to map them according to their level of interest in your plan and their influence or power over your plan. This will help to determine the best communication plan for each:

! COACH'S TIP

Coach's tip

When considering stakeholders, try to think broadly about who could possibly be involved or interested. This includes investors, senior management, the finance department, your line manager, the board, suppliers, customers/potential customers, your team, prospective employees, friends and family that you want to help you, etc.

	High	Interest	Low
High	**Involvement and participation** Stakeholdes that have a high level of interest and a good deal of power or influence over the plan should be heavily involved in the business planning process to ensure their buy-in. Discover their objectives early on, ensure they are included in your plan. Communicate regularly to keep them updated on progress to ensure they continue to support your plan.		**Communicate at a high level regularly** Stakeholders that have a low level of interest but are powerful or influential could at any time become more interested and start to interfere with your plans. Establish any objectives they have at the beginning of your planning process. Ensure you communicate at appropriate intervals with these stakeholders to give them assurance that there is no need for further involvement.
Influence/ Power Low	**Communicate key issues regularly** Stakeholders with a high level of interest but low power or influence, could become uncomfortable if they're not involved in the planning process and don't understand what is happening. While they have low power or influence on their own, if they become uncomfortable enough, could they band together to exert greater influence? Communicate key issues regularly to keep them happy.		**Minimal communication** Stakeholders with low interest and low influence really only need minimal communication to make them aware of any changes that may affect them.

Here's an example stakeholder map for a manager in a business proposing to introduce a new finance system:

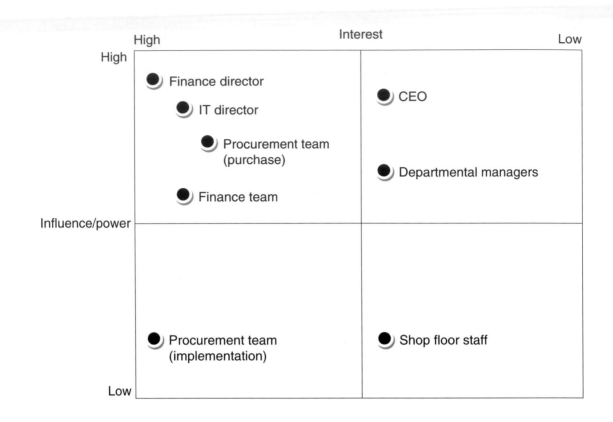

> **! COACH'S TIP**
>
> **Bespoke planning**
>
> It's important to treat each group separately. Although the generic advice given in the text above treats each stakeholder within a quadrant in a similar fashion, actually the communication plan for each stakeholder group will need to be different to take into account their information needs and also their preferred communication medium.

COMMUNICATION PLAN

Consider the following plan, which identifies the various stakeholders and their needs, and the best way to communicate with them.

Stakeholder group	Information needs	Communication medium
Finance director	Will set objectives for the new system	Face-to-face discussion to gather objectives
	Will authorize funding and allocate resources	Face-to-face presentation backed up with documented business plan
	Will want to oversee the implementation	Face-to-face progress updates backed up with a one-page project plan
IT director	Wants to set IT objectives	Face-to-face discussion to gather objectives
	Will allocate IT resources	Face-to-face workshop session to plan implementation with the IT team. Once plan is ready, present this face to face to the IT director with support from IT team.
Procurement team (purchase)	Will set commercial agreement objectives	Involved in planning process
	Will support with negotiation	Involved in negotiation process
Finance team	Directly affected by the implementation	Explain process in face-to-face meeting and gather their objectives and concerns. Identify an influential member of the team to be a key contact. Update via key contact at each stage of the implementation. Hold regular meetings to gather feedback. Involve individuals as required during implementation
Procurement team (implementation)	Will need to use the new system to raise purchase orders	Face-to-face presentation of plan and key benefits to them at the launch. Some email updates on progress. Face-to-face training on implementation
CEO	Interested in stability of business	Present key objectives of other stakeholders and outline plan at outset and gather any objectives. Short verbal update in board meetings monthly
Departmental managers and departmental staff	Interested in changes affecting their teams' processes	Join team meetings at outset to briefly outline plan and benefits. Cascade updates as part of regular team meetings. Face-to-face training for users on implementation
Shop floor staff	Will want to be aware of changes happening around the business	Cascade outline plan and benefits as part of a team meeting at outset and again on implementation

COACH'S TIP

Coach's tip

If in doubt, communicate far more than you think you need to!

COACHING SESSION 22

Yourstakeholder map and communications plan

Complete your stakeholder map and communications plan now:

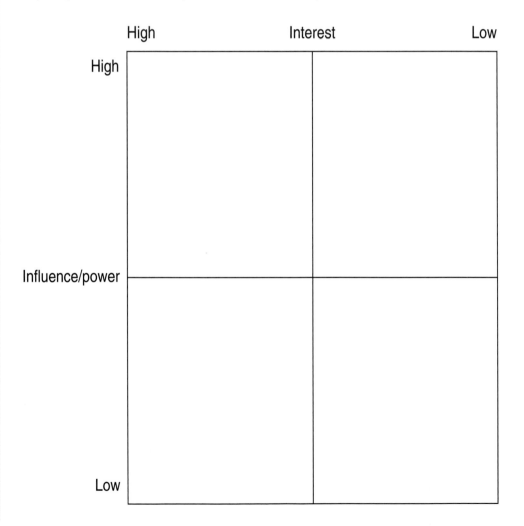

Stakeholder group	Information needs	Communication medium

ONLINE RESOURCE

Stakeholder mapping and communication plan

A downloadable stakeholder mapping and communication plan template can be found at:

www.TYCoachbooks.com/Businessplans

PRESENTING YOUR BUSINESS PLAN

The stakeholders involved in the initial presentation will have very different communication styles and personality traits. To appeal to each type, it's important to understand how they each think and what they'll find pleasing.

The following table shows a simple extract from a personality profile suggested by Merrill and Reid (see Bibliography), that you can use to try to assess people's different styles.

You'll recognize different qualities in yourself and people you know. People have a mix of these different qualities making up their personalities; however, most people will have preferences that lead them to behave more often in ways consistent with one or two of the styles listed below.

	Low assertiveness	High assertiveness
Low responsiveness	Analytical	Driver
High responsiveness	Amiable	Expressive

For the purposes of presenting a business plan, we'll look at each of these four styles and assume that people all have one predominant style. Providing you present to all the needs of all the styles, everyone in the room will see the information they need in the format they'd prefer, helping you to build rapport and giving you a greater chance of 'winning them over'.

Each of these personality types will have different communication styles and be interested in seeing your business plan in a different form. You need to ensure all of their needs are covered in your presentation and plan documentation.

Style	How to spot them	How to present your plan to them
Driver	Drivers are very direct. They'll use words like: plan, strategy, win, logical, objective and goals. They won't waste time with chit-chat; conversations will be structured and to the point. They'll want to understand the key points really quickly.	Produce an executive summary that summarizes all the key points from your business plan. When presenting your plan, talk to the Driver's needs first. Cover the key points on the first (few) slide(s) making sure the key financial figures (investment, payback, NPV) are quoted early on.
Expressive	Expressives like to look at the big picture and to be inspired. They'll use words like: flexible, spontaneous, emerging goals and innovation. They'll want to understand the vision for the business and what it will look and feel like in the future.	Talk to the Expressives next. Present your vision statement or mission statement, paint a picture of what the business will look and feel like in the future. Demonstrate your product and focus on how it's different from anything else on the market and how you will innovate in future to improve it further to appeal to new markets. In the business plan document, make sure you catch their eye with a picture of your product, or some visual representation of your plan – graphs of customer segments and needs, for example.
Amiable	Amiables are very people-focused. They'll use words like: collaborate, people, empathize and understand. They'll want to understand why people would buy, what needs you fulfil and how you'll work with partners.	Amiables are generally patient, so you can address their needs after the Drivers and Expressives. They will want to understand the people aspects of your plan. What are your objectives, how will you work with partners, and your team. what do you understand about your customers, how will you fulfil their needs? Demonstrate your product and focus on how people will use it and what it will mean to them; how will it make their lives easier?
Analytical	Analyticals are very practical. They'll use words like: evidence, common sense, detail, accurate and risk. They'll ask how it works; they'll spot problems and risks and ask how you'll overcome them.	Analyticals will want to see the detail of your plan. This will naturally fit towards the end of your presentation as you'll want to set the scene first before diving into the detail. They'll also want time to mull over the analysis. Let them have the full plan and presentation before the meeting, and ensure all the detail and analysis is clearly referenced into the appendices. Analyticals will need some convincing on how it will work. Make sure you have slides to cover your implementation plans and a risk register with mitigation plans.

NEXT STEPS

In this chapter you have:

- Mapped all stakeholders on the basis of how interested they are in your business plan and how much influence or power they have over your plan.

- Put together a communication plan for each stakeholder group, ensuring that all stakeholders buy-in to your plan.

- Understood the different communication styles of each stakeholder, and considered how to communicate not only what they need to know, but equally importantly, how they'd like to see that information.

In the next chapter you will go into more detail and think about tasks and timings. Which tasks are dependent on others? How will this affect your plan? It's time to look at the nitty gritty and really get things moving.

TAKEAWAYS

This is your opportunity to take stock of what you have learned from this chapter. You might now want to choose other chapters and exercises to focus on, or you can continue to work through the whole book if this better fits your needs.

Who are the key stakeholders in your business?

Which stakeholders are likely to support you and which may hinder?

Which stakeholders is it important to keep happy, to avoid them feeling the need to be too involved?

Do you have a personalized communication plan for each stakeholder group?

How do you feel about adapting your style to meet the communication styles of your different stakeholders?

IMPLEMENTING YOUR PLAN

✔ OUTCOMES FROM THIS CHAPTER

- In this chapter we'll develop some structured, detailed plans broken down into tasks and timings, to get your business opportunity up and running. It's important to have a detailed plan of activities so that:

  - you will be able to keep track of your actions and progress

  - you can be sure to start up on time

  - if your investors want to release funding in stages during the implementation (rather than releasing all the funding up front) they will be able to see a schedule to release funding against

  - you can keep your investors and other stakeholders appraised of progress compared to the plan.

It's important to have a detailed plan of activities, so that you are able to keep track of your actions and progress, not only to ensure you can start up on time, but also for your investors, who may agree to release funding at certain stages of the implementation (rather than releasing all the funding up front). If so they will want to see a plan and in addition, they'll want to see regular updates to see that you are sticking to the plan.

❗ COACH'S TIP

Keep investors on your side

Review your plan regularly with investors to retain their confidence and to ensure any staged payments of investments are not delayed.

COACHING SESSION 23

Implementing the plan

The first step is to list all the activities that you will need to undertake to get started; for example:

- get funding
- lease a property
- shopfit the property
- start marketing campaign
- contract with suppliers
- open the store

The next step is to break down each of these headings into specific tasks you need to do, to complete each.

1. Get funding
    a. Complete the business plan
    b. Present to investors
    c. Review contracts (get legal advice) and sign them
    d. Receive funding

2. Lease a property
    a. Define what you require from a property
    b. Research suitable areas for your property
    c. Contact agents and view properties
    d. Choose the property
    e. Get a survey
    f. Review the contract (get legal advice) and sign
    g. Move into the property

3. Shopfit the property
    a. Meet shopfitters
    b. Agree design and prices
    c. Choose shopfitter, review contract (get legal advice) and sign
    d. Complete the shopfitting

4. Start marketing campaign
    a. Meet advertising firms
    b. Design campaign and prices
    c. Choose advertiser, review the contract (get legal advice) and sign
    d. Start the campaign

Weeks: 1 2 3 4 5 6 7 8 9 10 11 12 13 14 15 16 17 18 19 20 21 22 23 24 25 26 27 28 29 30 31 32 33 34 35 36 37

1a 1b 1c 1d - funding received in stages over the life of implementation and beyond

2a 2b 2c 2d 2e 2f 2g

3a 3b - will not take this long, dependent on finding property 3c 3d

4a 4b 4c 4d - dependent on opening date

5a - will not take this long, dependent on opening day 5b 5c

6

Assumptions:

Need to have rough property costs (2a), shopfitting costs (3a), marketing costs (4a), supply costs (5a) to complete the business plan

Funding may be received in stages over the life of the implementation

Seach for funding can occur as soon as the business plan is ready, other research (property, marketing, supplies, etc.) can happen at the same time

Finalizing the shopfitting costs is dependent on choice of property

Completion of shopfitting is dependent on moving into the property

Marketing can only start once the property is chosen

The critical path is highlighted in light grey. Open day is dependent on finding the property and getting it shopfitted. All other activities have slack time built in.

5. Contract with suppliers

   a. Review suppliers

   b. Choose suppliers, review contracts (get legal advice) and sign

   c. Receive deliveries

6. Open the store

The third step is to put each of these activities into a timeline, noting that some are dependent on others, and therefore have to follow each other. The longest path of dependent activities is known as your critical path. For example, here there are many activities that can be done at the same time, for example talking to suppliers, searching for properties, talking to shopfitters. However, shopfitting cannot occur until you move into the property, so shopfitting is dependent on moving into the property:

The critical path is in finding the property and shopfitting it. All other activities have slack built in. If any activities on the critical path are delayed, the whole project will be delayed.

COACH'S TIP

Coach's tip

This plan was just typed into Microsoft Excel – you don't need a more complex project management package.

COACH'S TIP

Keep it on track

Review the plan regularly, mark off activities as they're completed, focus on the critical path to ensure nothing delays it.

→ NEXT STEPS

In this chapter you have:

- Broken down your plan into key headings and then into individual tasks under each heading.

- Written each activity on a timeline, paying particular attention to any activities that are dependent on the completion of another activity – these are put into the critical path.

In the next chapter you are going to review what you've learned from the business planning process, and hopefully from this identify ways in which you could improve next time. Continual review of your business is essential if you are going survive, and you will look at how you can build this in to your plans too, which will require you to continually update your plans as circumstances change.

TAKEAWAYS

This is your opportunity to take stock of what you have learned from this chapter. You might now want to choose other chapters and exercises to focus on, or you can continue to work through the whole book if this better fits your needs.

Do you need to break your plans down into any more detail here, to feel confident that you can manage the implementation?

Does your critical path fit into the time frames you originally imagined or do you need to review and amend your plans?

Will activities that are dependent on the completion of another task be a problem?

List here any additional resources that you need to complete your plan on time.

Where in your plan have you built in time for slippage, to cover unexpected events or problems?

12 WHAT HAVE YOU LEARNED FOR NEXT TIME?

✔ OUTCOMES FROM THIS CHAPTER

- In this chapter we'll first of all look at what you've learned from the business planning process. What would you do differently next time? We'll also look at the importance of continual review of your business to ensure you always stay ahead of new trends and avoid the traps that so many new businesses fall into.

Typically this is an area where both entrepreneurs and business managers are weakest. It's difficult to find time to continually review throughout implementation, but if you're so busy hacking your way through the jungle with a machete, then who is climbing a tree to make sure you're still going in the right direction, or even if you're in the right jungle! Furthermore after the plan is implemented it is even more difficult to find time to review how it went, after all, you're probably keen to get on with the next project! However, without a thorough review, you will lose all the learning from this implementation and you risk making the same mistakes next time.

! COACH'S TIP

Review your business plan

Throughout running your business, take time to review your business plan: what's changed in the outside world, what do you need to change to keep ahead of the competition?

COACHING SESSION 24

What have you learned from the business planning process?

Review your business planning process from inception to presentation and fill in the following questionnaire

What went well?

What didn't go so well?

What do you wish you'd done differently?

What will you do differently (be specific about how) next time?

WHAT ARE YOU LEARNING FROM RUNNING YOUR BUSINESS?

Throughout the implementation of your business plan it's important to review how things are going compared to your plan.

Review major milestones, review the financial performance compared to your budget, review your strategy and what changes to your strategy emerge as things change in the outside world.

In the introduction we discussed the reasons for business failure. Some of these are listed below, with some thoughts about why it's so important to continually review:

No business plan

Having a business plan is only the first step; what goes into the plan is based on assumptions about the future. Unless you continually review what's happening in the outside world, you could find yourself rigidly sticking to a plan that is no longer valid in the current environment. For example, if you are launching a new product, but a competitor develops something even better, you will need to react, not just continue with your now inferior product.

Lack of operating goals and objectives, and poor people management skills

Goals aren't just there to help you to plan your business, they're also there to help your staff, investors, customers, suppliers and other businesses you partner with to understand what you're trying to achieve. They are important for staff, to motivate and challenge them and to give them a guide for decision making.

Failure to measure goals and objectives

Goals will necessarily change over time. As you achieve them you'll need to set new goals or, as things change in the outside world, some of your goals may become unrealistic or irrelevant.

Measuring your activities and accomplishments against your goals helps you to stay motivated yourself, to see and measure progress and to identify quickly when things aren't going to plan so you can change your plans accordingly.

Recording your progress will give you evidence of a good track record of implementation if you have to gain more funding for future growth, or for your next business venture.

Failure to pay attention to cash flow

Poor management of cash flow is one of the biggest reasons for business failure. Banks and other lenders will want to see cash flow forecasts, but as things change over time and your investment requirements change, lenders will want to see that you've managed cash well in the past, in order to feel confident in lending in the future.

If you find you need a short-term loan or overdraft to cover short-term needs, for example a requirement for more working capital during growth, forecasting this well in advance will give you the opportunity to find a loan and negotiate a reasonable interest rate in plenty of time. If you wait until cash becomes a desperate need, you may be held to ransom with high interest rates, or worse still be unable to get funding!

> **! COACH'S TIP**
>
> Customer needs
>
> Survey your customers to gain early insight into their changing needs.

Failure to understand the industry and the target customer

Unless you continually review the environment and, more importantly, gather feedback from your customers, you may find that a competitor develops a product or service that solves your customers' needs better than yours does, or overcomes some disadvantage of your product, and overnight you lose your customer base.

All of these are important reasons to continually review progress.

> **! COACH'S TIP**
>
> Coach's tip
>
> Whilst we have focused on avoiding failure here, it is important to remember to celebrate our successes. Celebrate with customers, team members and partners to maintain morale and to take advantage of good PR (public relations).

COACHING SESSION 25

Top tips for continuous review

1. Set aside a substantial amount of your time to regularly review your business plan; carry out the same analysis you did as part of building the business plan in the first place, revise your plan and implement new ideas.

2. Develop a customer feedback sheet for all staff to keep and record information as they receive it.

3. Make it easy for customers to give feedback.

   a. Have a feedback section on your website.

   b. Email customers after purchase to solicit feedback.

   c. Set up surveys covering key areas of your offering and ask customers to complete them, then keep a track of statistics.

   d. Ensure you ask for freeform suggestions from customers, rather than only using a tick-box.

   e. Surveymonkey.com, Quicksurveys.com, freeonlinesurveys.com and Zoomerang.com all allow you to develop and use surveys free or at very low cost.

   f. If you're in a position to tender or pitch for business, each time you win or lose, ask for feedback:

      i. What did you do that the customer liked?

      ii. What did you do that the customer didn't like?

      iii. What did the competitors do better than you?

      iv. What did you do better than the competition?

      v. If there is one thing the customer wishes you did differently, what would it be?

4. Have weekly or monthly meetings to review customer feedback.

5. Develop a staff suggestion scheme. Rather than having a box in the corner for suggestions (which will not keep it at the forefront of people's minds), instead:

   a. Set competitions

   b. Have incentives for good ideas implemented

   c. Hold regular meetings and brainstorming sessions to gather ideas

6. Put in place a competitor tracking process.

   a. Regularly review what you can find out about what the competition are up to.

   b. Ask customers, shared suppliers and your sales team what they have discovered about your competitors.

   c. Conduct a regular news search and internet search on your competitors.

   d. Keep a log of what each competitor does, what changes they make; on reviewing the log, what links the actions they've taken, can you infer what their overall strategy is? If so, what would be the next obvious step for them?

! COACH'S TIP

What are the competition up to?

Track competitors actions, try to infer their strategy, try to imagine what they might do next.

→ NEXT STEPS

In this chapter you have:

- Thought about what went well and what you'd do differently next time throughout and at the end of the business planning process.

In the next chapter you will think about the future and how you might grow your business. This is both for yourself, but also if you plan to sell your business in the future, to make sure it is an attractive proposition.

TAKEAWAYS

This is your opportunity to take stock of what you have learned from this chapter. You might now want to choose other chapters and exercises to focus on, or you can continue to work through the whole book if this better your needs.

What would you say is the most important thing you've learned from the business planning process?

What are they key things you need to monitor to ensure your implementation isn't delayed?

What have you put in place to ensure that you avoid the common reasons for business failure?

In what ways did you not stick to your plan? Can you improve on this next time?

What is the one thing you will do differently next time?

13 | YOUR EXIT STRATEGY

- In this chapter we'll review how you might grow your business, what will make it attractive to future owners of the business and how to place a value on the business when you are ready to sell it.

HOW TO GROW YOUR BUSINESS

The first thing to consider is how to grow your business to an appropriate size in the early years.

If you're looking to sell the business in say five to ten years, you have just that long to get the business into an appropriate and attractive position for future potential buyers. You will need to grow rapidly to ensure that other competitors don't copy your idea and steal your potential market share.

There are a number of options for how to grow the business:

Options for growth	Advantages	Disadvantages
Organic growth: Build the business yourself, using your own funds, those of other investors or lenders and profits generated from the business.	This approach may give you a great deal of control over the opportunity, how it's grown and how it operates.	The disadvantage is that this approach is likely to be slower than other options. Bottlenecks will occur because of lack of funding or from how much growth you physically have the capacity to manage.
Acquisition: You could buy up competitors and mould them to your approach to grow more quickly.	This would be a very fast way to grow the business as each acquisition represents a sudden large increase in turnover.	Acquisitions are expensive; vendors will want to be compensated for loss of their income stream, so it's difficult to add value on top of a large acquisition price. Acquisitions are difficult to integrate; the acquired businesses will have their own systems, processes and culture which may not fit with your objectives. Planning for and managing an acquisition takes a great deal of management effort. Who will be running your existing business while your time is taken up?
Franchising: Once your first (or first few) branch(es) are running successfully, you can earn money by selling the franchise to other budding entrepreneurs and also earn royalties from the franchisees from ongoing sales.	This is a really fast way of growing the business. It earns you money each time you sell a franchise and on an ongoing basis from licence fees, keeping your cash flow positive.	You will have to be very organized to sell the franchise opportunity and to manage the franchisees to maintain your brand position. A franchised business may not be attractive to all potential buyers.
License your technology: If your business is based on a specific product or technology, you could license that product or technology for other competitors to use for a royalty fee.	If you don't have the capacity to satisfy the potential market, this is a really good way to make sure your product reaches all the customers who want it, rather than creating a need that competitors will find a way to fill. You will also increase your cash flow (from royalty payments) enabling you to grow further.	Negotiating licence agreements will be complex, so take legal advice.

$\longrightarrow$

Options for growth	Advantages	Disadvantages
Establish your business in one region leaving the future buyer to grow nationally.	Getting your brand known in a specific region may fend off competitors trying to steal and reuse your idea. It also leaves future buyers with an easy way to grow the business and add value.	National competitors may still see the benefits of your business idea and steal or adapt it for their own use nationally.

A key point is that you need to leave scope for the buyer to grow the business further. Why would anyone buy a business (where the acquisition price will reflect the current state of the business and its current ability to generate cash flow in the future) if they have no way to add value to the business themselves in the future?

It may be attractive to future buyers if you grow the business in one or more regions; document your implementation plans thoroughly, then sell just as you start to grow into a new region, thereby showing the buyer that the opportunity will work in the new region, but leaving them with a clear plan for growth that they can implement. This will potentially increase the price that you can command for the business sale.

Don't underestimate the need for acquirers to buy, however. Earlier in the book we reviewed the Technical Facilities Management industry. In this industry it is very hard to win new contracts other than on price, but shareholders want to see continual growth to add shareholder value. One of the easiest ways for existing TFM businesses to achieve that growth is to acquire small start-up businesses. It can be easier for an existing business to gain funding for an acquisition, than it is for them to take a short-term hit to profits by spending operating costs to set up new operations organically.

COACHING SESSION 26

Look at the competition

- Review your larger competitors:
- What actions are they taking?
- What strategy can you infer from their recent actions?
- Does acquisition seem to be a key theme?
- Where are they acquiring?
- What types of core competencies are they buying in when they acquire?
- Does this make your business an attractive addition to their portfolio?

Write your findings below.

VALUING YOUR BUSINESS FOR SALE

The value of your business is the sum of the net asset value plus goodwill.

Net assets, remember from Chapter 8, is the Balance Sheet value for total assets less total liabilities; i.e. everything your business owns less anything it owes. Remember that the assets have all been depreciated in the Balance Sheet over their lives, so there may be some assets, for example buildings, that are worth more in the real world than the Balance Sheet value would show.

> **! COACH'S TIP**
>
> **Get a survey!**
>
> Have properties re-valued by a RICS qualified surveyor if you feel that the Balance Sheet is undervaluing property.

There are a number of simple and more complex methods for valuing a business's goodwill. In the main, they all rely on establishing current profits or net cash flows and projecting them out for a number of years.

EBITDA MULTIPLE VALUATIONS

One very common approach is to take EBITDA (earnings before interest, tax, depreciation and amortization – review the Profit and Loss Account shown in Chapter 7 for a reminder) and forecast it forward for a number of years. The method of forecasting it forward is simply to apply a multiple; a figure to represent how many years you expect to generate these profits, this would be called an EBITDA multiple.

For example, the latest EBITDA for our business ABC Ltd illustrated in Chapter 7 was £300k. If the EBITDA multiple for this industry is 6 (see box below on establishing the correct EBITDA multiple), then £300k × 6 = £1.8m

As you can see this is quite a rough calculation; it's not a true accurate valuation, as for each business the true forecast of future cash flows is dependent on how fast the business grows, external influences such as market demand, actions of competitors, etc. and of course the time value of money (see Chapter 8). However, I would recommend using this method as a first step, to estimate the rough ballpark valuation.

ESTABLISHING THE CORRECT EBITDA MULTIPLE

How do we establish what is the correct multiple to apply to the EBITDA? In Chapter 8 in the section Evaluate the Opportunity under Net Present Value, we looked at the time value of money and we discounted future cash flows into today's money terms.

Remember the discount table? Looking at the discount factor at 12% for ten years, the tenth-year cash flow was discounted to 0.322 of its face value. If you had actually forecast your cash flows to the best of your ability for the next ten years, each cash flow for each year would have been discounted more and more until the tenth-year's cash flow is stated at 32% of its face value. From this you can see that when using a multiple, it's likely to be lower than 10. So you can expect to sell your business for less than 10 times its EBITDA plus net assets. What the actual multiple is will depend on your industry, how much growth potential there is, how competitive the industry is, and many other factors.

Merger and acquisition firms that help buyers and vendors to do deals will place a great deal of value on their own method for calculating a multiple for any business in any industry. However, as we're looking for a rough ballpark valuation at this stage, we can take a shortcut.

There are plenty of reports and statistics published online about actual acquisitions, the prices paid compared to the EBITDA, so we can estimate the multiple for any industry using this information.

ONLINE RESOURCE

EBITDA resources

Take a look at:

http://pages.stern.nyu.edu/~%20adamodar/New_Home_Page/datafile/vebitda.html

http://www.grantthornton.com.au/files/dealtracker_2013.pdf

http://www.finexpert.info/capital-market-data/multiples/evebitda.html

or simply search for EBITDA Multiples on your search engine to find the latest data.

Take the EV*/EBITDA multiple quoted for your industry, take your EBITDA from your latest Profit and Loss Account, multiply the two together and you have your very rough business value.

*EV is Enterprise Value, the amount paid to acquire a business. EV/EBITDA therefore shows us how many times more the acquirer paid to acquire the business, than the EBITDA earned by that business.

More accurate valuation methods

A more accurate way to value the goodwill, once you've actually made the decision to put the business up for sale, is to forecast the future cash flows to the best of your ability.

Your starting point will be your net cash flow for the last financial year (and your most up to date forecast for this year's net cash flow – containing actual cash flows for the months to date plus forecasts for the months up to year end).

COACHING SESSION 27

Cash flow forecast

Complete the cash flow forecast in Chapter 8 (downloadable from www.TYCoachbooks.com/Businessplans). Starting with Time 1, fill in the cash flow forecast for the current year. Now complete each Time based on what you would do with the business for the next ten years if you continued to run it:

- What impacts do you expect to see from competitors' actions?

- What market trends have you identified to date and how will these impact future cash flows?

- Would you invest for future growth, what would this cost? And what benefits would it bring in future years?

Once you've completed the spreadsheet, the Net Present Value calculated is today's value of the goodwill of the business. Don't forget to add the Net Asset Value from the Balance Sheet (they will also be buying the assets and the liabilities of the business). Don't forget to adjust property values if you've had a RICS valuation showing that your buildings are worth more than the Balance Sheet valuation.

The discount factor you choose to use to calculate the NPV will depend on the acquirer's standards. If in doubt 12% is a reasonable discount factor to use. However, the discount factor will affect the valuation significantly – try a few different discount factors in the spreadsheet now to get a feel for the sensitivity. The lower the discount factor used, the higher the value for your business.

Of course, this is only your valuation of the business. The true value of any business is the amount an acquirer is prepared to pay for it. Everything we've discussed in this chapter is for you to get a ballpark valuation, but in reality, your potential buyers will also calculate their own valuations and the final price if agreed, will be dependent on your negotiation with the buyer.

→ NEXT STEPS

In this chapter you have:

- Reviewed options for how to grow your business, and considered the best approach for your opportunity to achieve your objectives.

- Looked at establishing a value for your business ready for negotiating its sale.

In the next and final chapter there is a sample business plan for you to look at, compare your own with, and if you prefer, you can download it and over-type it with your own information.

TAKEAWAYS

This is your opportunity to take stock of what you have learned from this chapter. You might now want to choose other chapters and exercises to focus on, or you can continue to work through the whole book if this better fits your needs.

What are your plans for the future of your business?

How will you achieve those objectives?

What values did you calculate for your business using each of the methods shown?

EXAMPLE BUSINESS PLAN

✔

- In this chapter there is a full business plan laid out in our suggested format for you to review, learn from and, if you prefer, you can download it and type over it to ensure that you have covered all the necessary sections and included all the pertinent information required to complete your business plan.

SCHOOL-LEAVER-OPOLY: BUSINESS PLAN

🖱 ONLINE RESOURCE

Example business plan

This business plan is available to download at:

www.TYCoachbooks.com/Businessplans

CONTENTS

EXECUTIVE SUMMARY

The opportunity

An opportunity exists to develop and sell a board game (and an 'app' version) aimed at recent and prospective school leavers, college students, apprentices and undergraduates to help them with the management of personal finances.

The vision and our core competency

We make managing personal finances fun and easy for all young people with the aim of improving the debt management of the UK as a whole. Making learning fun, appealing and easy to apply.

Who are we?

Jane Doe (Director):   Qualified Accountant and experienced Learning Professional

John Doe (Director):   Experienced business to business Sales Executive

David Doe (Part time resource): Experienced Digital Marketing Executive

Who will buy our game?

Schools, colleges, large companies with a substantial apprentice intake, recruitment consultancies specializing in apprentice places and parents.

We intend to partner with a range of charities, government departments, teaching unions and industrial unions, to garner marketing support and communications.

We will sell online via our own website, eBay and Amazon plus using a Sales Executive to approach charities, government departments, teaching unions, schools, colleges, businesses, industrial unions, etc.

What's different about our game?

It's fun and competitive, people will want to play.

Learning can take place at home with parents, at school or college with friends or on your own via the app.

People can play again and again to reinforce the learning.

THE FINANCIALS

For an up-front investment of just £12,000, this profitable, cash-generating opportunity pays back in the first year and gives a Net Present Value (over ten years at 12%) of £72,000 from a highly prudent set of assumptions.

The exit strategy

The plan is to grow the business in the UK for up to five years, selling both the board game version and an app version to schools, colleges and direct to parents, then to sell the business to an existing games company.

THE DETAILED PLAN

The mission and business objectives

We make managing personal finances fun and easy for all young people with the aim of improving the debt management of the UK as a whole; our specific business objectives are to:

- Make learning appealing and fun, delivered directly and easily transferable to people's personal lives.

- Appeal to parents to ensure they encourage their children to play and, supported by guidance/advice for parents and education professionals, to ensure key learning points are discussed.

- Build the business to a reasonable size for sale within five years, leaving scope for future owners to grow the business further.

- Partner with government departments, charities and teaching unions and industrial unions to gain marketing support.

For more detail and analysis, see Appendix 1.

Our USP

The game is fun and competitive so it's more engaging than a training course and will lead to word of mouth recommendations and can be played many times to reinforce the learning, unlike a classroom course.

Learning can happen anywhere, it's not restricted to the classroom and being so affordable will appeal to a wide range of markets: colleges, schools, businesses with apprenticeships as well as the home audience.

For more detail and analysis, see Appendix 2.

Market analysis

Approximately one million people turn 16 each year in the UK, providing a consistent annual market for School-Leaver-Opoly. Given the need to use a workbook during the game, consistent sales of additional workbooks will ensure continuous sales opportunities with existing owners.

The UK Government has a stated policy to 'help young people develop their character, a sense of belonging and the behaviours which help them succeed in learning, work and life', so we believe we can gain support from the Department for Education (DFE) to publicize the game to schools and colleges.

Parents are supporting children longer into their lives, whether in work or training, they will be keen to encourage children to budget responsibly.

There are currently no existing games in this space, we have registered designs and copyright and we are in the process of developing an 'app' version of the game to ensure we don't lose out on market share from competitors.

We intend to market to schools, colleges, universities, companies with a large apprentice intake, recruitment consultants specializing in apprentice recruitment and parents.

There are almost 4,300 schools and colleges in the UK; we have very prudently built our business plans on selling one game to 10% of these per year for five years, then also selling 30 workbooks per game sold per year.

For more detail and analysis, see Appendix 3.

Reaching the customer

We have an internal sales professional on the board approaching the DFE, pfeg (personal finance education group), teaching unions (NUT, NASUWT, ATL), industrial unions, etc. to gain marketing support.

We have a website developed already, linked directly to our manufacturer's website to make ordering simple and to gather feedback after each sale.

We are also selling via Amazon and eBay with an Amazon affiliate link on our website, again to make ordering simple.

We have a social media campaign underway already, with YouTube video clips linked to all websites and social media to demonstrate the game.

For more detail and analysis, see Appendices 4 and 5.

Resourcing

Apart from the two directors and part-time digital marketing assistant, all resourcing is hired on a temporary basis or outsourced to specialist companies, in order to make the business completely scalable so that fluctuations in demand are easily managed with no fixed cost burden to affect profitability.

For more detail and analysis, see Appendix 6.

The plan

Our plan, which is already underway, includes:

- Registering designs.
- Approaching potential partner organizations, setting up NDAs and contracts (with legal assistance).
- Putting together a sales plan for approaching potential customer organizations.
- Developing a final version of the game, workbook and short demo to run with customers to gain interest.

- Producing video webclip of demo to use in online advertising, YouTube, etc.
- Approaching online game designer (approaching colleges/universities for help – use student game designers?)
- Putting plans in place for future growth options re other versions of the game.
- Developing the marketing plan in detail.
- Developing sales and development plans, allocating time carefully between development, sales and demo/running sessions.
- Setting up Ltd company online.
- Launching marketing campaign at education exhibitions, e.g. Education Show/Education Innovation, etc.

For more detail and analysis, see Appendices 7 and 8.

Key risks identified were mitigated as follows:

Risk	Description of risk (what is it? when would it occur? what would be the impact on the opportunity?)	Our mitigation plans to overcome the risk
1.	Competitor launches similar product with greater marketing investment	Big splash launch Partner with charities, DFE, pfeg, etc. Register designs
2.	Hasbro sues for design breach	Re-name (without 'opoly') – this was only the working title! Ensure all designs sufficiently different – take design registration advice There are existing games utilizing this format; Make-Your-Own-Opoly, Farm-Opoly, Pirate-Opoly, etc. Research copyright issues fully
3.	Competitor launches online/app version	Bring forward online and app design – to be ready on launch of board game
4.	Get the marketing wrong	Attack as many channels as possible using a range of marketing messages, to ensure it appeals to the target audience
5.	No partners to support us	Approach them early, link our game to their stated objectives, make it easy for them administratively – question them extensively on their needs/views/issues and provide solutions
6.	Poor media reviews	Test (and redesign) the product extensively with the target audience to gain positive reactions. Invite media to launch/demos, etc.
7.	Poor customer reviews	Continuously gather feedback from customers (education, industry and end users) to gain insights into how to improve the product

For more detail and analysis, see Appendix 9.

The financials

Financial Evaluation of School-Leaver-Opoly — Discount factor: 12%

Description	0	1	2	3	4	5	6	7	8	9	10	Total
Cash Inflows												
Sales of board games	0	8600	8600	8600	8600	8600	8600	8600	8600	8600	8600	
Sales of workbooks	0	860	1720	2580	3440	4300	4300	4300	4300	4300	4300	
Sales of apps		9900	9900	9900	9900	9900	9900	9900	9900	9900	9900	
Total additional cash inflow	0	18500	19360	20220	21080	21940	22800	22800	22800	22800	22800	215100
Cash Outflows												
Develop board game	0											
Develop first version simple app	5000											
Improve & redesign app			10000									
Register trade marks, copyright, designs	1000											
Marketing Investments:												
- digital marketing	5000	500	500	500	500	500	500	500	500	500	500	
- web design	0											
Manufacturing set up	1000											
Manufacturing costs		4300	4300	4300	4300	4300	4300	4300	4300	4300	4300	
Total additional cash outflow	12000	4800	14800	4800	4800	4800	4800	4800	4800	4800	4800	70000
Net cash flow	−12000	13700	4560	15420	16280	17140	18000	18000	18000	18000	18000	
Cumulative cash flow	−12000	1700	6260	21680	37960	55100	73100	91100	109100	127100	145100 *	
Discount Factor	1	0.893	0.797	0.712	0.636	0.567	0.507	0.452	0.404	0.361	0.322	
Net present value	−12000	12232	3635	10976	10346	9726	9119	8142	7270	6491	5796	71733
Internal rate of return												
Return on investment	121%											100%
	14510 / 12000											
Benefit : Cost	215100 / 70000											
	3.1 / 1											

205

Assumptions built into the financial evaluation

The assumptions listed below are highly prudent, at all stages we've used the lowest possible sales figures and highest cost estimates for low volume production.

- Quotes for app design range from £500 upwards. Given the complexity, we estimate £5k.

- Digital marketing paid for at a rate of £500 per day for design and set-up.

- Quote for manufacturing received is highly volume dependent, from £10 per game for 1,000 to £4 for 10,000.

- 4,300 schools and colleges: we aim to sell one game each to 10% in first year, growing to 50% by year 5 at £20.

- 30 workbooks sold per game each year at £2 each.

For more detail and analysis, see Appendix 10. Full implementation plan is in Appendix 11 and slides to support this presentation are in Appendix 12.

Appendices and detailed analysis follow.

APPENDICES – ANALYSIS AND DETAIL

APPENDIX 1: PERSONAL AND BUSINESS OBJECTIVES

Once you've decided whether each objective is essnetial or desirable, rank the desirable ones out of 10; the essential ones are by definition 10/10.

Personal objectives/ personal 'must-nots'	Essential/ Desirable	Desirable objectives ranked out of 10	Consequential business objectives
To improve the management of personal finances for young people in the UK.	E		The delivery method must be appealing and fun to ensure learning. The learning must be directly and easily transferable to people's personal lives.
To ensure young people learn effectively, making the learning fun and making it stick!	E		Take-up must be extensive, to have the desired impact. It should be appealing to parents, so they encourage their
To have a large impact on financial responsibility of UK citizens.	D	6/10	children to play and are happy to join in and play with the children to ensure key learning points are discussed. Marketing and route to customers will be key, to ensure rapid take-up.
To build a business to sell on to a larger company in five years.	E		Need to build the business quickly to a size attractive to potential acquirers, but leaving plenty of scope for further growth. Investors need to be aware of exit strategy; financials need to be carefully planned to ensure a fair return to all parties. Build rapidly in the UK, to allow the future owner scope for international expansion.

Not to get involved in selling directly to consumers.	D	8/10	Need to get a partner on board to spread the word, for example: Skills Funding Agency, pfeg (personal finance education group), Prince's Trust, etc.
			Could sell directly to colleges or universities or larger companies with a substantial apprentice intake.
			Gain Government support (Dept of Education).
Not to manufacture in-house.	D	8/10	Find suppliers/partners/ outsourced manufacturing provider.

SCHOOL-LEAVER-OPOLY MISSION STATEMENT:

We make managing personal finances fun and easy for all young people with the aim of improving the debt management of UK citizens in general.

APPENDIX 2: SCHOOL-LEAVER-OPOLY USP

Capabilities	Differentiation	Benefits	Questions for customers	Points of interest for stakeholders
A fun way to learn.	Being a competitive game, it's more engaging than a training course.	Young people will want to play, no 'selling' required by parents, teachers or employers.	How important is it to you that your child/student *wants* to learn?	Word of mouth marketing as young people share their experiences.
Learning can happen anywhere: school, home, with family, friends or learning providers.	Boxed and portable containing guidance for parents or educators to make it simple to run.	No travel to a course. Young people can learn with their friends and share learning.	To parents: Would you like to be involved in your child's learning? To educators: Is it important to have a standard, consistent, simple-use learning tool?	Broad market appeal – schools, colleges, larger companies with apprentice intake, as well as home use – two versions available (home version and commercial version?)
Affordable.	An easy purchase decision.	Suitable for all budgets.	To parents: What would it be worth to you to prepare your child for going out into the world? To educators: What other options do you have within your budget?	Good volume sales are achievable with few customer objections – easy for the customer to try it out.
Can be used many times for refresher on learning.	Unlike a training course, outcomes are different each time, so there's always more to learn.	Repetition will reinforce learning.	To parents: Do you think your child will need a few practices to get the message? To educators: Is it important to you to be able to refresh/revise?	Through multiple use, there is an opportunity to sell replacement workbooks (each player works through a book to plan & budget, etc.)

SCHOOL-LEAVER-OPOLY CORE COMPETENCY:

Making learning fun, appealing and easy to apply.

APPENDIX 3: MARKET ANALYSIS

Approximately one million people turn 16 each year in the UK, providing a consistent annual market for School-Leaver-Opoly. Given the need to use a workbook during the game, consistent sales of additional workbooks will ensure continuous sales opportunities with existing owners.

Political	The UK Government has a stated policy to 'help young people develop their character, a sense of belonging and the behaviours which help them succeed in learning, work and life' (HM Government Positive for Youth).
Economic	Economic downturn and living standards – makes personal financial management more important than ever.
Sociological	Young people staying in education, training or work. Parents supporting children's finances for longer – including home buying.
Technological	More games available online or via apps now. More financial advice accessible online.
Legal/Regulatory	No patents available for board games – only protection available is to register designs – more complex? Difficult to defend?
Ecological	Paper and plastic materials not ecologically friendly, negatively affects customer perception?

Force	Analysis	Potential Response
Threat of new entrants	Existing board game manufacturers could easily develop a competitive product.	Register designs. Extensive launch marketing rapid to ensure School-Leaver-Opoly becomes the favoured brand. Partner with supportive government departments, charities, etc. to gain recognition quickly.
Threat of substitute products	Online version of the game. Training courses.	Need to develop online game quickly? Develop 'training course in a box' version of the game for commercial providers and license it out ('training in a box' meaning it contains everything the educator needs: the game, trainer notes to guide them through the game, etc.).
Bargaining power of suppliers	Main supplier is manufacturer.	Source alternative suppliers to maintain ability to negotiate.

→

Force	Analysis	Potential Response
Bargaining power of buyers	Wide range of buyers – schools, colleges, companies. Could buyers form a group to negotiate prices in bulk?	Keep the game affordable. Bulk purchases would actually help with volume/sales growth.
Competitive rivalry	No current provider of this specific product; however, games manufacturing is a highly competitive market with very few companies.	Important to be ready to sell the business – start negotiations with competitors early?

APPENDIX 4: THE CUSTOMER

Customer group	Why would they buy?	**A**ttention and **I**nterest	**D**esire (answer 'why would they buy?')	**A**ction (make it easy to try)
Schools/ colleges/ universities/ companies with a large apprentice intake	To help students with life skills.	Gain support/ marketing/comms from DFE, pfeg, teaching unions (NUT, NASUWT, ATL), industrial unions, etc. Research debt statistics for young people.	Research school and college, teaching union and companies objectives/mission statements, identify pastoral care statements and 'people' statements and link to them.	Produce a 'training in a box version' with tutor session plans and guidance. Keep it affordable. Run some pilot sessions (will need trained support).
Recruitment consultancies specializing in large-scale apprentice recruitment	To differentiate their apprentices as more rounded individuals.	Research debt statistics for young people.	Provide a compelling case for differentiation.	Run the game for them, no effort or administration required.
Parents	To help their children.	Gain support/ marketing/comms from DFE, pfeg, etc. or from schools, colleges, etc. Research support and financial deals for young people – include these in the game – e.g. discounts on council tax for people on apprentice schemes, young people under 25 who get funding from the Skills Funding Agency or Young People's Learning Agency, etc.	Provide compelling vision of financially stable children vs children requiring financial support.	Affordable, internet ordering, parent support booklet included.

APPENDIX 5: DELIVERY

Market channel	Benefit	Drawback	Solution
Internal sales team	Control, dedicated team, knowledgeable sales people, good customer contact and information gathering. Sales exec is a partner in the business, so motivated and knowledgeable.		
Web sales (own website)	Wide reach, automated process, low cost, marketing through social media.	Website development and maintenance, less opportunity to get customer feedback.	Link to manufacturer's ordering site, to make ordering simple, gather feedback after each sale.
Web sales (through intermediary – e.g. eBay shop, Amazon affiliation, etc.)	Wide reach, automated process, low cost, take advantage of their marketing effort.	Fees/commissions charged reduce your margin.	
Social media	Low cost, easy to manage yourself, could 'go viral' and attract a lot of attention.	Your message may be lost in the plethora of other content, no way of targeting who sees your message.	Use Digital Marketing Professional to help with design of comms.

APPENDIX 6: INTERNAL RESOURCES

Function	Requirements
Quality	Strict standards with outsourced manufacturers Robust, simple, trainer instructions for trainers, parents, etc.
Finance	See financial sections later in this business plan
IT	Online game/app game developer required
Logistics	eBay/Amazon shop linked directly to outsourced manufacturer
Marketing	Seek support from DFE, pfeg, Prince's Trust, teaching unions, etc.
Sales	Web sales, sales executive on commission to approach schools, colleges, etc.
HR	Sales exec is partner in business. Self-employed: web designer, online game/app designer
Operations	Mainly outsourced manufacturing, distribution, etc. Game design completed and updated by Jane Doe. Customer communications, feedback, etc. sought by Jane Doe
Procurement	Outsourced manufacturers' agreements

APPENDIX 7: SWOT

Opportunities	Threats
Partnership with SFA, DFE, pfeg, Prince's Trust, teaching unions	Ineffective or insufficient marketing leads to slow take up
3900 secondary schools in UK	Competitor board game companies develop a rival version with better marketing comms, steal market share
391 colleges in UK	
Sales of workbooks for new students to use after sales of initial board games	Need to manage internal priorities: not to spend so much time delivering the game/training to impinge on selling and development activities
Online/app version	
New versions of games in the future for commercial enterprises to cover other key skills; business finance, interpersonal skills, etc.	Amazon selling at a discount may impact our brand value

Strengths	Weaknesses
A great format for a board game	No online/app game development experience
Engaging and fun	
Covers key learning points	No legal knowledge for NDAs, contracts, etc.
Ongoing sales of workbooks after initial board games sold	
Sales exec is a partner in the business	
Experienced digital marketing professional on board on temporary/part-time/as needed basis (a relative)	

APPENDIX 8: STRATEGIC OPTIONS

Review the SWOT analysis above, list all the options available to you to take up the opportunities, overcome the threats, use your strengths, and overcome your weaknesses:

STRATEGIC OPTIONS TO MANAGE SWOTS

- Register designs.
- Approach potential partner organizations, set up NDAs and contracts (get legal assistance).
- Put together sales plan for approaching potential customer organizations.
- Develop final version of the game, workbook and short demo to run with customers to gain interest.
- Produce video webclip of demo to use in online advertising, YouTube, etc.
- Approach online game designer (approach colleges/universities for help – use student game designers?).
- Put plans in place for future growth options re other versions of the game.
- Develop marketing plan in detail.
- Develop sales and development plans, allocate time carefully between development, sales and demo/running sessions.
- Set up Ltd company online.
- Launch marketing campaign at education exhibitions, e.g. Education Show/Education Innovation.

APPENDIX 9: RISK ANALYSIS

High   Impact   Low

High	
● Competitors design similar product and 'out-market' our offering	
● Hasbro (owner of Monopoly) sues for design breach	
● Competitor develops online/ app version	

Probability

● Get the marketing wrong and no-one buys it	
● No companies/unions/govt depts/charities interested in partnering with us	
● Poor reviews in the media affect sales	

Low

Risk	Description of risk (what is it, when would it occur, what would be the impact on the opportunity?)	Your mitigation plans to overcome the risk
1.	Competitor launches similar product with greater marketing investment	Big splash launch Partner with charities, DFE, pfeg, etc. Register designs
2.	Hasbro sues for design breach	Re-name (without 'opoly') this was only the working title! Ensure all designs sufficiently different – take design registration advice. There are existing games utilizing this format: Make-Your-Own-Opoly, Farm-Opoly, Pirate-Opoly, etc.
3.	Competitor launches online/app version	Bring forward online and app design – to be ready on launch of board game.
4.	Get the marketing wrong	Attack as many channels as possible using a range of marketing messages, to ensure it appeals to the target audience.
5.	No partners to support us	Approach them early, link our game to their stated objectives, make it easy for them administratively – question them extensively on their needs/views/issues & provide solutions.
6.	Poor media reviews	Test (and redesign) the product extensively with the target audience to gain positive reactions. Invite media to launch/demos/etc.
7.		Continuously gather feedback from customers (education, industry and end users) to gain insights into how to improve the product.

APPENDIX 10: THE FINANCIALS

Competitor Analysis

Section	Analysis of the situation
Sector	Hasbro: stable sales, small increases in assets.
	Other competitors: varied results.
	This market is polarized, one or two huge players (Hasbro being the biggest) and a plethora of much smaller specialist companies.
	Many of the big games names you'd know from your childhood have been bought by Hasbro.
	Hasbro: the largest portion of costs are in the manufacture and distribution of games.
Company(s)	There are a massive range of providers, price competition appears to be based on comparative prices and value in use.
	There are a huge range of competitors with a large range of games each, there seems to be a great deal of innovation in this market.
	Those competitors that manufacture their own games have a reasonably high investment in fixed assets, but of the smaller competitors there seems to be a mix between those that manufacture themselves and those that outsource, reducing their asset investments considerably.
Information available	Very little published information on strategy, etc. Smaller providers are completely exempt from publishing reports and Hasbro, being global, is not realistically a head-on competitor. However, despite spending a great deal on product development themselves, they do also pay considerable royalties, which implies they are interested (or have been in the past) in buying ideas from other companies. They also have a history of acquisition.
Ratios	See below.
Evaluation	This appears to be a profitable, cash-rich sector, with opportunities for growth.

Ratios for Hasbro

Unfortunately, most UK board games manufacturers are small and exempt from filing accounts, but at least we can get some general idea of costs from Hasbro, albeit a much larger organization which will necessarily have very different cost structures and economies of scale.

Ratio	Calculation	Hasbro	
		2012	2011
Profitability on Sales			
Gross margin	$\dfrac{\text{gross profit}}{\text{annual sales}} \times 100$	59%	57%
Royalties	$\dfrac{\text{royalties}}{\text{annual sales}} \times 100$	7.4%	7.9%
Product development	$\dfrac{\text{product dev}}{\text{annual sales}} \times 100$	4.9%	4.6%
Advertising	$\dfrac{\text{advertising}}{\text{annual sales}} \times 100$	10.3%	9.6%
Expenses	$\dfrac{\text{expenses}}{\text{annual sales}} \times 100$	46%	43%
Net profit margin	$\dfrac{\text{net profit}}{\text{annual sales}} \times 100$	8%	9%
Return on Investment			
Return on Capital Employed (ROCE)	$\dfrac{\text{net profit}}{\text{total equity plus long-term loans}} \times 100$	6%	7%
Measures of efficiency			
Stock days	$\dfrac{\text{stock}}{\text{cost of sales}} \times 365$	69 days	66 days
Debtor days	$\dfrac{\text{debtors}}{\text{sales revenue}} \times 365$	91 days	88 days
Creditor days	$\dfrac{\text{creditors}}{\text{cost of sales}} \times 365$	31 days	27 days
Liquidity ratios			
Quick ratio	$\dfrac{\text{current assets} - \text{stock}}{\text{current liabilities}}$	1.5	1.3
Risk			
Gearing	$\dfrac{\text{long-term loans}}{\text{total equity plus long-term loans}} \times 100$	24%	25%

Evaluate the opportunity

Financial Evaluation of School-Leaver-Opoly	Discount factor:	12%										
Description						Time						
	0	1	2	3	4	5	6	7	8	9	10	**Total**
Cash Inflows	0											
Sales of board games		8600	8600	8600	8600	8600	8600	8600	8600	8600	8600	
Sales of workbooks		0	860	1720	2580	3440	4300	4300	4300	4300	4300	
Sales of apps		9900	9900	9900	9900	9900	9900	9900	9900	9900	9900	
Total additional cash inflow	0	18500	19360	20220	21080	21940	22800	22800	22800	22800	22800	**215100**
Cash Outflows												
Develop board game	0											
Develop first version simple app	5000											
Improve & redesign app			10000									
Register trade marks, copyright, designs	1000											
Marketing Investments:												
- digital marketing	5000	500	500	500	500	500	500	500	500	500	500	
- web design	0											
Manufacturing set up	1000											
Manufacturing costs		4300	4300	4300	4300	4300	4300	4300	4300	4300	4300	
Total additional cash outflow	12000	4800	14800	4800	4800	4800	4800	4800	4800	4800	4800	**70000**
Net cash flow	-12000	13700	4560	15420	16280	17140	18000	18000	18000	18000	18000	
Cumulative cash flow	-12000	1700	6260	21680	37960	55100	73100	91100	109100	127100	145100 *	
Discount Factor	1	0.893	0.797	0.712	0.636	0.567	0.507	0.452	0.404	0.361	0.322	
Net present value	-12000	12232	3635	10976	10346	9726	9116	8142	7270	6491	5796	**71733**
Internal rate of return												100%
Return on investment	14510	**121%**										
	12000											
Benefit : Cost	215100	70000										
	3.1	1										

Assumptions built into the evaluation

The assumptions listed below are highly prudent; at all stages we've used the lowest possible sales figures and highest cost estimates for low-volume production.

- Quotes for app design range from £500 upwards; given the complexity, we estimate £5k.

- Digital marketing paid for at rate of £500 per day for design and set-up.

- Quote for manufacturing received is highly volume dependent, from £10 per game for 1,000 to £4 for 10,000.

- 4300 schools and colleges, aim to sell one game each to 10% in first year, growing to 50% by year 5 at £20.

- 30 workbooks sold per game each year at £2 each.

Annual Budget for School-Leaver-Opoly

Description							Time						
Income	Jan	Feb	Mar	Apr	May	Jun	Jul	Aug	Sep	Oct	Nov	Dec	Total
Sales of board games			300	500	800	1000	1000	1000	1000	1000	1000	1000	8600
Sales of workbooks													0
Sales of apps				300	700	1000	1100	1200	1200	1300	1400	1700	9900
													0
													0
													0
Total Income	0	0	300	800	1500	2000	2100	2200	2200	2300	2400	2700	18500
Expenditure													
Develop board game	0												0
Develop first version of app	2500	2500											5000
Improve and redesign app													0
Register trade marks, designs, etc.		1000											1000
Digital marketing		450	450	450	450	450	450	450	450	450	450	500	5000
Web design	0												0
Manufacturing set up	1000												1000
Manufacturing costs		150	250	400	500	500	500	500	500	500	500	500	4800
													0
Total Expenditure	3500	4100	700	850	950	950	950	950	950	950	950	1000	16800
Net Profit	-3500	-4100	-400	-50	550	1050	1150	1250	1250	1350	1450	1700	1700

APPENDIX 11: IMPLEMENTATION PLAN

The critical path for implementation is highlighted in darker grey. Until manufacturing is set up and commences, there is nothing to deliver to customers.

Manufacturing set-up includes a first run of prototype games, that can be used for demonstration, sales effort and filming the YouTube clips.

Everything needs to be ready for the Education Show running in week 13 of our plan.

Some partners are on-board already, meetings are booked with more prospective partners in the first month of our plan.

	Already Complete	Weeks 1	2	3	4	5	6	7	8	9	10	11	12	13	14	15
Develop board game	■															
Develop app		■	■	■	■	■	■	■	■							
Register trade marks etc	■															
Digital marketing							■	■	■	■	■	■	■	■	■	■
Web design																
Manufacturing set up		■	■	■	■											
Manufacturing									■	■	■	■	■	■	■	■
Deliver to customers										■	■	■	■	■	■	■
Gain partnership support	■	■	■	■	■											
Sales effort							■	■	■	■	■	■	■	■	■	■
Run workshops								■	■	■	■	■	■	■	■	■
Webclip on YouTube							■	■	■							
Education show														■		

APPENDIX 12: BUSINESS PLAN PRESENTATION SLIDES

School-Leaver-Opoly

Business Plan

The opportunity

- An opportunity exists to develop and sell a board game (and an 'app' version) aimed at recent and prospective school leavers, college students, apprentices and undergraduates to help them with the management of personal finances.

Mission statement

- We make managing personal finances fun and easy for all young people with the aim of improving the debt management of the UK as a whole. Making learning fun, appealing and easy to apply.

Introducing the team

- Jane Doe (Director):
  Qualified Accountant and experienced
  Learning Professional

- John Doe (Director):
  Experienced business to business Sales
  Executive

- David Doe (part-time resource):
  Experienced Digital Marketing Executive

Who will buy our game?

- Schools, colleges, large companies with a
  substantial apprentice in-take, recruitment
  consultancies specializing in apprentice
  places, and parents.

- We intend to partner with a range of
  charities, government departments, teaching
  unions and industrial unions, to garner
  marketing support and communications.

- We will sell online via our own website,
  eBay and Amazon plus using a Sales
  Executive to approach Charities, Government
  Departments, Teaching Unions, Schools,
  Colleges, Businesses, Industrial Unions, etc.

The financials

- For an up-front investment of just £12,000,
  this profitable, cash generating opportunity
  pays back in the first year and gives a net
  present value (over ten years at 12%) of
  £72,000 from a highly prudent set of
  assumptions.

Risks and mitigation plans (1)

Risk	Description of risk (what is it, when would it occur, what would be the impact on the opportunity?)	Mitigation plans to overcome the risk
1	Competitor launches similar product with greater marketing investment	Big splash launch Partner with charities, DFE, pfeg, etc. Register designs
2	Hasbro sues for design breach	Re-name (without "opoly") this was only the working title! Ensure all designs sufficiently different – take design registration advice. There are existing games utilising this format; Make-Your-Own-Opoly, Farm-Opoly, Pirate-Opoly, etc.
3	Competitor launches online/app version	Bring forward online & app design – to be ready on launch of board game

Risks and mitigation plans (2)

4	Get the marketing wrong	Attack as many channels as possible using a range of marketing messages, to ensure it appeals to the target audience
5	No partners to support us	Approach them early, link our game to their stated objectives, make it easy for them administratively – question them extensively on their needs/views/issues & provide solutions
6	Poor media reviews	Test (and redesign) the product extensively with the target audience to gain positive reactions. Invite media to launch/demos, etc.
7		Continuously gather feedback from customers (education, industry and end users) to gain insights into how to improve the product

A Demonstration

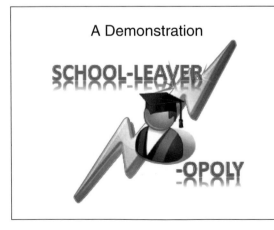

SCHOOL-LEAVER -OPOLY

ACTION PLAN

Make a note here of the top five key things you hadn't previously considered:

1.

2.

3.

4.

5.

List your objectives below. Each objective should be SMART:

- Specific – it is clear *exactly* what you will do

- Measureable – so that you will find it easy to determine when you are finished

- Achievable – it may be stretching and you may need support or advice, but it is do-able

- Relevant – it moves you closer to achieving your overall goals

- Time-bound – so that you can make sure you're still on track for starting your new opportunity within the time frames you set

	Objective	What's the first step?	Who's support do you need?	How will you know when it's good enough?
1				
2				
3				
4				
5				

Now let's consider *how* you will approach these objectives. This section is about your behaviours as well as specific tasks. For example, you might decide to keep moving through the steps methodically, to be more persistent and tenacious, to stop procrastinating as well as listing the specific tasks you want to get completed.

What will you...	... keep doing?	... do more of?	... do less of?
Tomorrow			
This Week			
This Month			
This Year			

Insert your Implementation Plan from chapter 11 here.

COACH'S TIP:

Keep your action plan somewhere you can see it at all time, on your office wall for example, review it regularly to keep you engaged and on track.

QUICK HELP GUIDE

This quick help guide summarizes the key points from each chapter of the book. Why not photocopy it and put it on your notice board as a handy reference as you go through your business planning process?

Chapter 1: Why are you doing this?
- Establish your personal objectives – you don't want to work really hard to build a business then find that it doesn't satisfy you. What do you want out of the opportunity for yourself? What do you *not* want to happen?

- Use your personal objectives to set your business objectives. For example, if you want to be in control of your own destiny, you'll need to ask yourself how you can fund your business without giving any control over to partners or investors and then consequently, will it make your growth slower if your investment capital is restricted?

- Write a mission statement to attract and inform partners, investors, suppliers, customers and potential employees.

Chapter 2: Who will want your product or service?
- Establish your unique selling propositions (USPs) to ensure you can differentiate yourself from your competitors. Write questions to ask customers to establish their needs and to guide you as to which USPs to discuss in depth with customers that will be of interest to them.

- Write out your core competency; this will help you to fulfil customers' needs better by adding value to your proposition and it will also give you opportunities for growth and diversification in the future by using that competency in different markets.

Chapter 3: What is the state of the market?
- How big is the market – and how much of the market is it realistic for you to take in what time frames?

- Complete a PESTLE (Political, Economic, Sociological, Technological, Legal/Regulatory, Ecological) review of the environment as it affects your business now, and in the medium and long term, to ensure you have plans to react to changes in the outside world.

- Look at the Five Forces in your market place (competitive rivalry, new entrants, substitute products, suppliers and buyers) to establish what threats you face and how to overcome them.

- Use this information to complete the Opportunities and Threats section of a SWOT analysis.

Chapter 4: Getting your product to your customer
- Use AIDA (Attention, Interest, Desire, Action) to plan your marketing campaign.

- Use many routes to market: traditional ones (sales team, etc.) and modern methods (social networking) to ensure you reach the right target audience.

Chapter 5: How will you organize yourself?
- Use QFILMSHOP (Quality, Finance, IT, Logistics, Marketing, Sales, HR, Operations, Procurement) to plan how you will organize your business.

- Then use this information to pull together the Strengths and Weaknesses section of your SWOT analysis.

- Brainstorm as many strategic options for taking up each opportunity, overcoming each threat, using your strengths and building on your weaknesses as you can. Evaluate each option on its ease, speed, cost-effectiveness, appeal. Build the best options into your business plan.

Chapter 6: The risks
- Brainstorm all the risks you can think of; categorize them by their impact on your idea and the likelihood of them happening. Now you can put together appropriate plans to overcome each risk.

Chapter 7: Understanding the financials
- Make sure you understand the financial statements of your:

    - Competitors – for benchmarking performance and double checking your assumptions about costs

    - Customers – can they afford to pay you?

    - Suppliers – will they be around to supply you in the long term?

- Use SCIRE analysis (Sector, Company, Information available, Ratios, Evaluation) to ensure you see the big picture (where are these companies going) not just the current situation.

Chapter 8: The financials – evaluate your business opportunity and manage your business
- Evaluate your opportunity using Benefit:Cost, Payback, NPV and IRR to ensure your investors or senior managers have all the information they need to make a decision.

- Produce a budget and cash flow to help you to manage your business and to be able to share information with investors or senior managers to give them confidence in your management.

- Forecast and monitor your working capital requirements carefully; poor cash management is the number one reason for business failure!

Chapter 9: Gaining funding

- Evaluate what funding you need and separate out the long-term requirements from the short term so that you get appropriate funding for different needs.

Chapter 10: Presenting your plan

- Map your stakeholders to establish how interested they are in your idea and how much power or influence they have over it. Create a communications plan to keep them happy at all stages.

- Consider the communication styles of your stakeholders to ensure that you not only present the right information, but that you present it in the right way to engage and convince them.

Chapter 11: Implementing your plan

- List all the activities you need to undertake to get started, then break these down into each specific task under each heading.

- Take each of these and draw them into a time-line showing which activities are dependent on the completion of others to establish your 'critical path'.

- Monitor your actions against the plan to ensure your critical path is not delayed.

Chapter 12: What have you learned for next time?

- Review your learning for next time: What went well? What didn't go so well? What would you do differently next time?

- Find ways to invite customer feedback; ensure it is collected and reviewed. Change your operations to suit your customers' needs.

- Don't fall into the common traps:
    - no business plan
    - lack of operating goals and objectives and poor people management skills
    - failure to measure goals and objectives
    - failure to pay attention to cash flow and lack of attention to accounts receivables and inventory
    - failure to understand the industry and the target customer.

Chapter 13: your exit strategy

- Begin with the end in mind.

- If you want to grow a sustainable business to leave as a legacy, how will you grow? Organically? By acquisition? Through franchising or licensing?

- If you want to sell, in five years' time, what will be attractive about your business to a potential acquirer?

BIBLIOGRAPHY

Introduction

FinancialPreneur.com 2008, taken from: Business start-ups and closures: VAT registrations and de-registrations – 2007, results published in December 2008 on http://www.statistics.gov.uk

Mike Pendrith for Performance Point Corporation, 2013: http://www.performancepoint.ca

Chapter 1: Why are you doing this?

Tony Hseih, *Delivering Happiness*, Business Plus – Hachette Book Group. 2010

Chapter 2: Who will want your product or service?

Peter C. Fusaro and Ross M. Miller, *What went wrong at Enron?*, John Wiley & Sons Inc. 2002

Patrick Barwise and Sean Meehan, *Simply Better*, Harvard Business School Press. 2004

USP definer adapted from the DVP (Differentiated Value Proposition) by TACK International

Chapter 3: What is the state of the market?

Michael E. Porter. 'The Five Competitive Forces that Shape Strategy', *Harvard Business Review*, 2008

MCi UK Facilities Management Market Research Report. 2013

Chapter 8: The financials—evaluate your business opportunity and manage your business

Finance for Managers, Harvard Business School Publishing Corporation. 2002

Martha Amram and Nalin Kulatalaka, *Real Options*, President and Fellows of Harvard College. 1999

Chapter 10: Presenting your plan

D. W. Merrill and R. H. Reid, *Personal styles and effective performance*, New York: CRC Press. 1999

Chapter 14: Example business plan

HM Government Positive for Youth (a new approach to cross-government policy for young people aged 13 to 19) Ref DFE-00133-2011

INDEX